This book belongs to:

_____

LEISURE ARTS, INC.
Little Rock, Arkansas

EDITORIAL STAFF

Vice President and Editor-in-Chief: Anne Van Wagner Childs. *Executive Director:* Sandra Graham Case. *Editorial Director:* Susan Frantz Wiles. *Publications Director:* Carla Bentley. *Creative Art Director:* Gloria Bearden. *Senior Graphics Art Director:* Melinda Stout. PRODUCTION — *Managing Editor:* Susan White Sullivan. *Senior Editor:* Andrea Ahlen. *Project Coordinators:* Carol Bowie Gifford, Joyce Scott Holland, and Jennifer S. Potts. DESIGN — *Design Director:* Patricia Wallenfang Sowers. EDITORIAL — *Managing Editor:* Linda L. Trimble. *Associate Editor:* Janice Teipen Wojcik. *Assistant Editors:* Tammi Williamson Bradley, Terri Leming Davidson, and Stacey Robertson Marshall. *Copy Editor:* Laura Lee Weland. ART — *Book/Magazine Graphics Art Director:* Diane M. Hugo. *Senior Graphics Illustrator:* Stephen L. Mooningham. *Graphics Illustrators:* Faith R. Lloyd, Fred Bassett, and Linda Culp Calhoun. *Photography Stylists:* Pam Choate, Sondra Daniel, Karen Hall, Aurora Huston, Courtney Frazier Jones, and Christina Myers. PROMOTIONS — *Managing Editors:* Alan Caudle and Marjorie Ann Lacy. *Associate Editors:* Steven M. Cooper, Dixie L. Morris, Jennifer Ertl Wobser, and Marie Trotter. *Designer:* Dale Rowett. *Art Director:* Linda Lovette Smart. *Production Artist:* Leslie Loring Krebs. *Publishing Systems Administrator:* Cindy Lumpkin. *Publishing Systems Assistant:* Susan M. Gray.

BUSINESS STAFF

Publisher: Bruce Akin. *Vice President, Marketing:* Guy A. Crossley. *Vice President and General Manager:* Thomas L. Carlisle. *Retail Sales Director:* Richard Tignor. *Vice President, Retail Marketing:* Pam Stebbins. *Retail Marketing Director:* Margaret Sweetin. *Retail Customer Service Manager:* Carolyn Pruss. *General Merchandise Manager:* Russ Barnett. *Vice President, Finance:* Tom Siebenmorgen. *Distribution Director:* Rob Thieme.

CREDITS

PHOTOGRAPHY: Ken West, Larry Pennington, Mark Mathews, Karen Shirey, and David Hale, Jr., of Peerless Photography, Little Rock, Arkansas, and Jerry R. Davis of Jerry Davis Photography, Little Rock, Arkansas. COLOR SEPARATIONS: Magna IV Color Imaging of Little Rock, Arkansas. CUSTOM FRAMING: Nelda and Carlton Newby of Creative Framers, North Little Rock, Arkansas. PHOTOGRAPHY LOCATIONS: The Empress of Little Rock Bed and Breakfast, Little Rock, Arkansas, and the homes of John and Janice Choate, Charles and Peggy Mills, Duncan and Nancy Porter, and Dr. Reed and Becky Thompson.

Library of Congress Catalog Number 97-75961
International Standard Book Number 1-57486-104-2

INTRODUCTION

Steeped in folklore and aged customs, our most beloved holidays are celebrated with a kaleidoscope of seasonal symbols. From love-struck Cupids to genial Santas, unforgettable images from many countries and eras brighten our holiday traditions. This volume, with inspiration from vintage cards and memorabilia, introduces an exclusive collection of stitched treasures to enrich this ever-evolving holiday legacy. Our colorful montage of festive finery features elegant framed pieces that remind us of the reason for each season with reverence or mirth. You'll also find exquisite linens, eye-catching pillows, cozy afghans, and casual wear that's too lovely and versatile to pack away when the holiday is past. With each stitch of these masterful pieces, another thread is added to the magnificent tapestry of holiday lore and legend, creating a priceless heritage for generations to come as we become fashioners of holiday reverie.

TABLE OF CONTENTS

VALENTINE'S DAY

*T*ender and romantic, Valentine's Day finds young sweethearts dreaming of lacy greetings with sentimental rhymes, beribboned candy boxes, and long-stemmed rosebuds. On this idyllic occasion, warmhearted cherubs aim arrows tipped with enchantment, and Victorian poets ponder the boundless dimensions of love.

Charts on pages 48-49 and 51

𝔸dorning a beautiful bow pillow, Cupid patiently awaits prospective suitors. Pristine linen accessories are embellished with luscious red roses entwined about scrolled initials. The monogrammed pieces promise to become cherished heirlooms.

Chart on page 51

Charts on pages 52-53

9

ST. PATRICK'S DAY

Revered over the ages for its lush natural beauty, mystical Ireland evokes images of leprechauns, lace, and a legendary patron saint. Centuries after his passing, St. Patrick's feast day is observed with ever-present shamrocks and vivid shades of green. Celtic blessings steeped in wit and wisdom add a lyrical touch to the Emerald Isle's rich heritage.

Charts on pages 54-55

EASTER

Easter, a renewal of heart and soul, comes to pass as the earth awakens from its seasonal repose. While ardent choirs glorify the risen Lord, furry bunnies and newborn chicks welcome a world bright with budding flowers, tinted eggs, woven baskets, and vibrant bows.

Charts on pages 56-58

Chart on pages 56-57

14

*An invigorating warmth, filling the air with a sense of
anticipation, heralds the ethereal joy of Easter and springtime.
Eggs, chicks, and bunnies, symbolizing the profusion of tender
young life, give homage to our Savior's rebirth.*

Charts on pages 58 and 59

Charts on pages 60 and 61

16

*A*wake, thou wintry earth —
Fling off thy sadness!
Fair vernal flowers, laugh forth
Your ancient gladness!
Christ is risen.

— THOMAS BLACKBURN

Chart on page 61

Charts on page 61

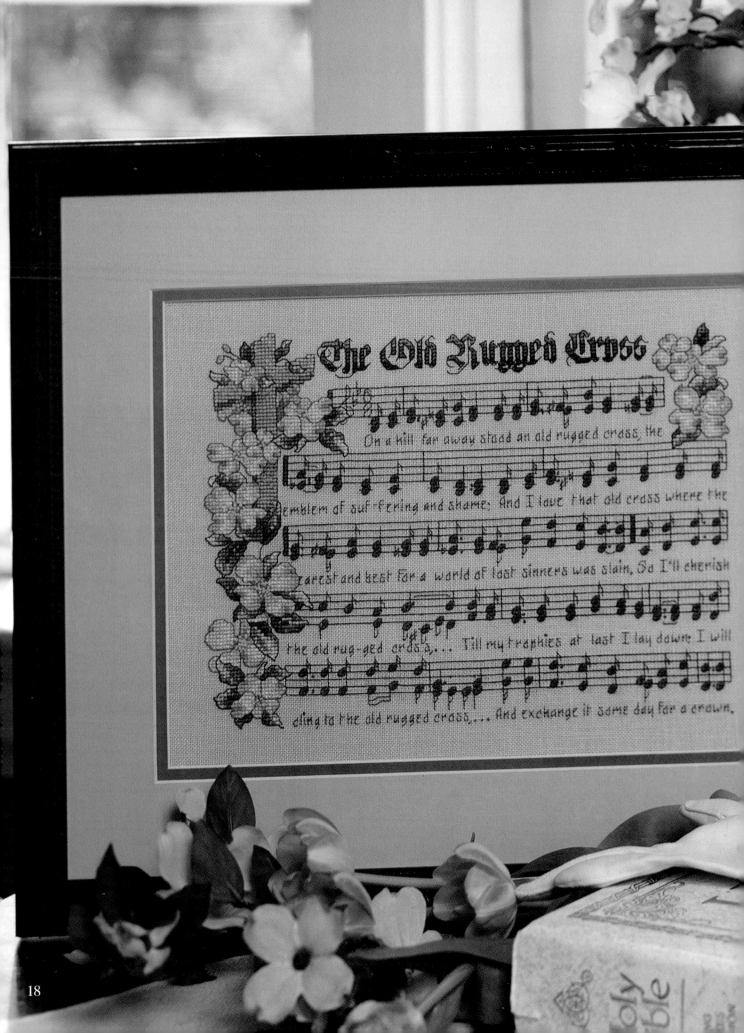

Graceful dogwood blossoms accent the beloved lyrics of this century's most popular and widely published hymn, producing a beautiful reminder of Easter's spiritual nature.

Chart on pages 62-63

19

INDEPENDENCE DAY

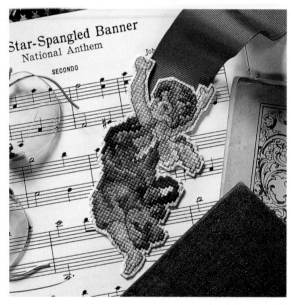

Grand and majestic, the American flag has been the cornerstone of Independence Day celebrations through peace and war, feast and famine. Old Glory became indelibly linked with hope and perseverance when Francis Scott Key penned "The Star-Spangled Banner" in 1813. For decades since, this anthem has united singers with patriots of ages past who consecrated the Stars and Stripes with word and deed.

Chart on pages 64-65

Rooted in rugged pioneer resourcefulness, the Early American spirit is kept alive in homey heirlooms such as quilts and samplers. Enduring patterns from this rich heritage impart a touch of history to a patriotic pillow and embroiderer's notions.

Chart on pages 66-67

Chart on pages 66-67

*The man who loves home best,
and loves it most unselfishly,
loves his country best.*

— J. G. HOLLAND

Chart on pages 66-67

hALLOWEEN

Mirth and mystery surround
Halloween, a time when ordinary
encounters take on a delightful air
of frightfulness. Dusky shadows
transform docile kittens and playful
pumpkins into spine-tingling spirits,
and clouds crossing the moon awaken
visions of cackling witches sailing on
weatherbeaten brooms. According to
legend, even the smoke from a snuffed
candle acquires special powers on
All Hallow's Eve — the ability to
foretell prosperity or woe.

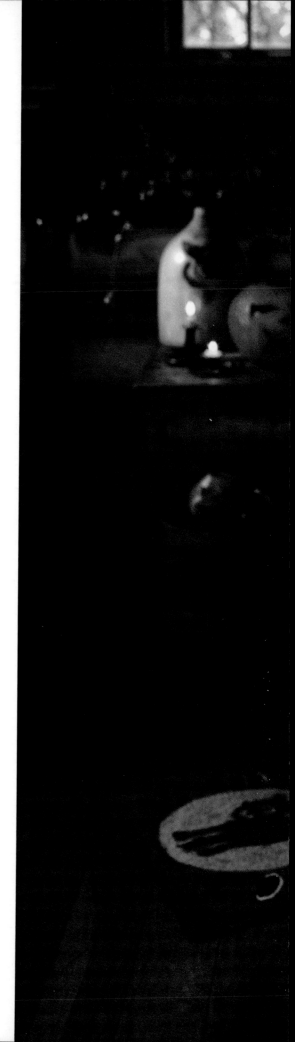

Charts on pages 68-69 and 75

When the moon is full and crops are ripe, field pumpkins come to life! With our senses on edge, the snap of a twig arouses heart-stopping fancies of gap-toothed gourds, witches in high-buttoned shoes, and ink-black cats guarding bristly brooms.

Chart on pages 70-71

Charts on pages 72-73

Chart on page 76

Charts on pages 74-76

A Hallowe'en merry, a Hallowe'en bright,
Though pumpkins make faces and ghosts walk at night,
Let no noises scare you, and don't start to run,
For 'tis but a joke, and Hallowe'en fun.

— FROM A VINTAGE POSTCARD

Chart on page 74

Charts on page 72

30

Snuggly garments displaying wily witches, jittery jack-o'-lanterns, and brooding black cats capture the engaging charm of our Halloween heritage. Join in the madcap merriment by embellishing your wardrobe with hair-raising creatures of the night.

Chart on pages 68-69

ThANKSGIVING

C herished for its tranquillity and abundance, the Thanksgiving season offers a chance to meditate on the countless blessings bestowed on our families and this nation. When our Pilgrim forefathers celebrated their newfound prosperity with friends and relatives, they passed on a noble heritage, a harvest table overflowing with good food and good cheer.

Charts on pages 78 and 80-81

33

*G*athered together, we thank our Heavenly Father for the year's bountiful yield. Fill your home with praise to the Lord, who enriches our fields, by displaying the rich images of this feast on your tables and walls.

Chart on page 84

Chart on pages 80-81

34

Chart on pages 82-83

*Now thank we all our God,
With hearts and hands and voices,
Who wondrous things hath done,
In whom His world rejoices.*

— MARTIN RINKART

Charts on page 79

Chart on page 78

Chart on pages 82-83

37

Charts on page 79

38

Chart on page 84

Energized by brisk autumn breezes and scampering leaves, bustling farmers race to collect their crops in time for Thanksgiving. Ever grateful for warmth and shelter, we emblazon our cool-weather wardrobe with mementos of this glorious season.

Charts on page 79

CHRISTMAS

A time that is both reverent and festive, Christmas finds a jubilant world eager to shake off its wintry slumber and rejoice in our Savior's birth. The Yuletide, wrapped in a magical aura of innocence and wonder, centers on family traditions, celebrations of faith, and childhood fantasies. In our glorious glimpse of Santa, cherubs watch over the rosy-cheeked patriarch making his Christmas Eve rounds with greatly anticipated treasures.

Charts on pages 86-87 and 92

Charts on page 90

*Pretty poinsettias, adoring angels, and jolly Santas
are unmistakable signs of the holiest and merriest of seasons.
Throughout the house, we acknowledge this holiday
with lovely handmade trimmings.*

Chart on page 91

Chart on pages 88-89

*Christmas angels grace a covered album holding dear memories
of holidays past. The awesome marvel of the Babe's lowly birth,
the essence of Christmas, is captured beautifully as ever-vigilant
angels and an adoring mother venerate the swaddled Child.*

Chart on page 93

In hopes that St. Nicholas soon will arrive, we deck the walls and don colorful holiday sweaters. The spirit of Christmas is kept alive with the help of a handsome Santa puffing on his proverbial pipe and a festive flower to brighten stark winter snows.

Chart on page 85

46

Charts on pages 85 and 91

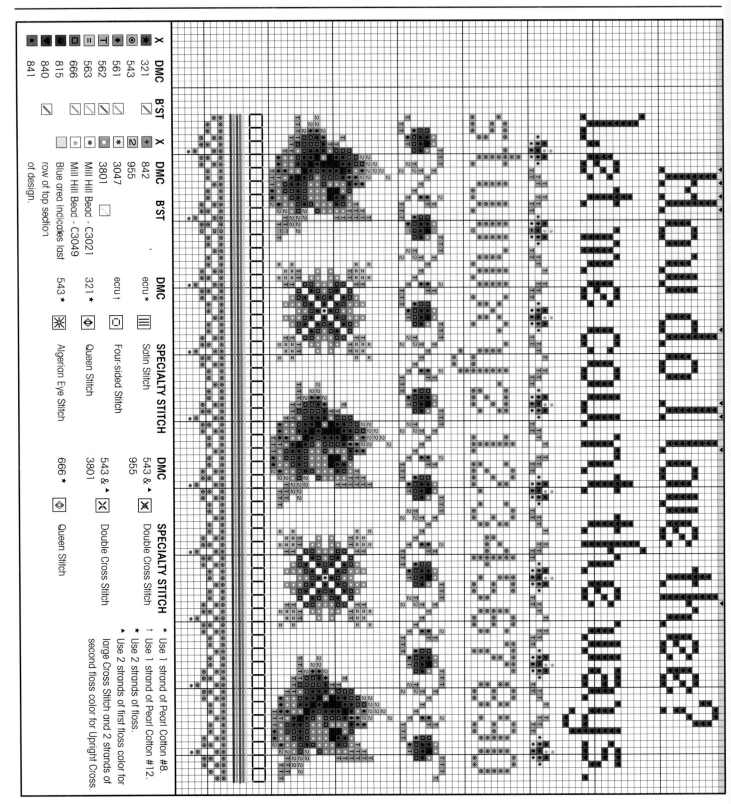

X	DMC	B'ST
▨	321	◹
◨	543	◹
◧	561	
◼	562	◹
‖	563	◹
⊤	666	◹
◆	815	◹
◉	840	
▨	841	◹

X	DMC	B'ST
▢	842	
•	955	
◈	3047	
2	3801	
✱		

Mill Hill Bead - C3021
Mill Hill Bead - C3049
Blue area indicates last
row of top section
of design.

	SPECIALTY STITCH	DMC	B'ST
‖‖‖	Satin Stitch	ecru *	
▢	Four-sided Stitch	ecru †	
◈	Queen Stitch	321 ✱	
❋	Algerian Eye Stitch	543 ✱	

	SPECIALTY STITCH	DMC	B'ST
❈	Double Cross Stitch	543 & ▲	❈
✖	Double Cross Stitch	955	
✖	Double Cross Stitch	543 & ▲	✖
◈	Queen Stitch	3801	
◈	Queen Stitch	666 ✱	

* Use 1 strand of Pearl Cotton #8.
† Use 1 strand of Pearl Cotton #12.
✱ Use 2 strands of floss.
▲ Use 2 strands of first floss color for
large Cross Stitch and 2 strands of
second floss color for Upright Cross.

"How Do I Love Thee?" Sampler in Frame (shown on page 7): The design was stitched over 2 fabric threads on a 14" x 20" piece of Antique White Belfast Linen (32 ct). Two strands of floss were used for Cross Stitch and 1 strand for Backstitch. Refer to chart for type of thread and number of strands used for Specialty Stitches. See Specialty Stitch Diagrams, page 50. Attach cream beads using 1 strand of DMC 543 floss and red beads using 1 strand of DMC 321 floss. See Attaching Beads, page 95. Personalize and date sampler using DMC 543 floss and alphabet and numerals from chart. It was custom framed.

Design by Linda Culp Calhoun.

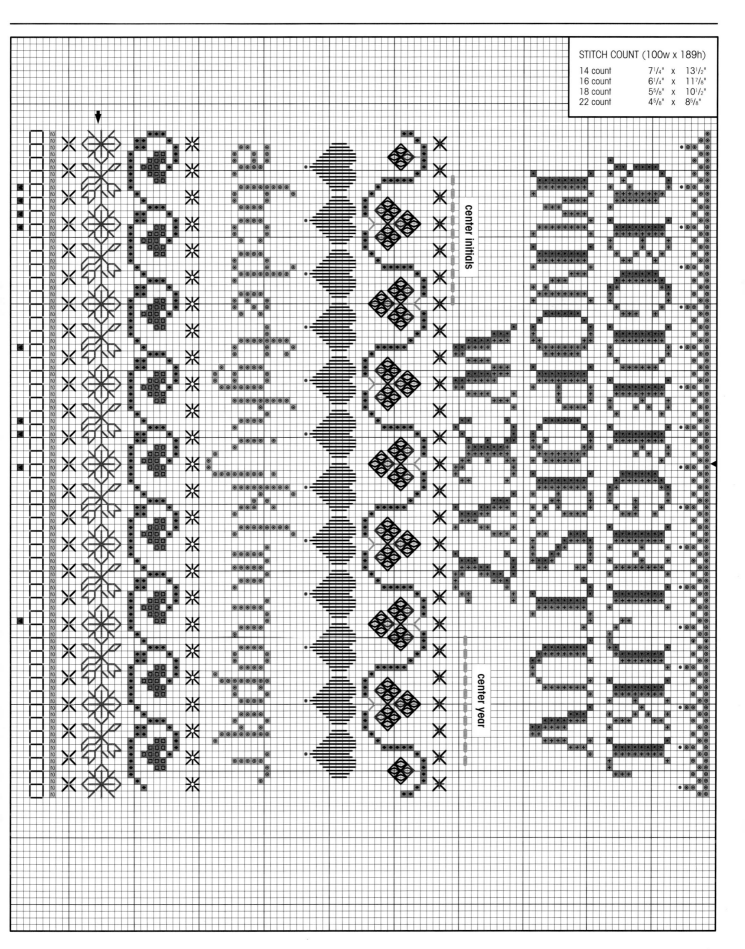

STITCH COUNT (100w x 189h)

count	width		height
14 count	7¼"	x	13½"
16 count	6¼"	x	11⅞"
18 count	5⅝"	x	10½"
22 count	4⅝"	x	8⅝"

center initials

center year

VALENTINE'S DAY

"How Do I Love Thee?" Sampler in Frame (shown on page 7, chart on pages 48-49): Refer to chart for type of thread and number of strands to use for Specialty Stitches.

SPECIALTY STITCH DIAGRAMS
(**Note:** Bring threaded needle up at 1 and all odd numbers and down at 2 and all even numbers.)

PULLED STITCHES
When working Pulled Stitches, fabric threads should be pulled tightly together to create an opening in the fabric around the stitch. Figs. show placement of stitch but do not show pulling of the fabric threads. Keep tension even throughout work.

Algerian Eye Stitch: An "eye" is formed in the center of this stitch. Come up at 1, go down in center, and pull tightly toward 3. Come up at 3, go down in center, and pull tightly toward 5; continue working in this manner until stitch is complete (stitches 5-15) (**Fig. 1**). Work row of Algerian Eye Stitches from right to left.

Fig. 1

Four-sided Stitch: This continuous stitch is worked from left to right. Come up at 1 and pull tightly toward 2; then go down at 2 and pull tightly toward 1. Work stitches 3-14 in same manner (**Fig. 2**). Continue working in the same manner to end of row.

Fig. 2

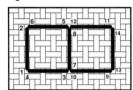

EMBROIDERY STITCHES
Double Cross Stitch: This decorative stitch is formed by working four stitches. Work large Cross Stitch (stitches 1-4) as shown in **Fig. 3**; then work Upright Cross (stitches 5-8) over center of large Cross Stitch (**Fig. 4**). The top stitch of the Upright Cross must be made in the same direction on all Double Cross Stitches worked.

Fig. 3

Fig. 4

Queen Stitch: This decorative stitch forms a diamond shape. Work a long stitch (stitch 1-2) loosely and catch with a short stitch (stitch 3-4) (**Fig. 5**). Complete stitch (stitches 5-16), catching each long stitch with a short stitch as shown in **Figs. 6-7**.

Fig. 5

Fig. 6

Fig. 7

Satin Stitch: This stitch is a series of straight stitches worked side by side (**Fig. 8**). The number of threads worked over and the direction of stitches will vary according to the chart.

Fig. 8

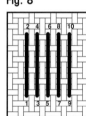

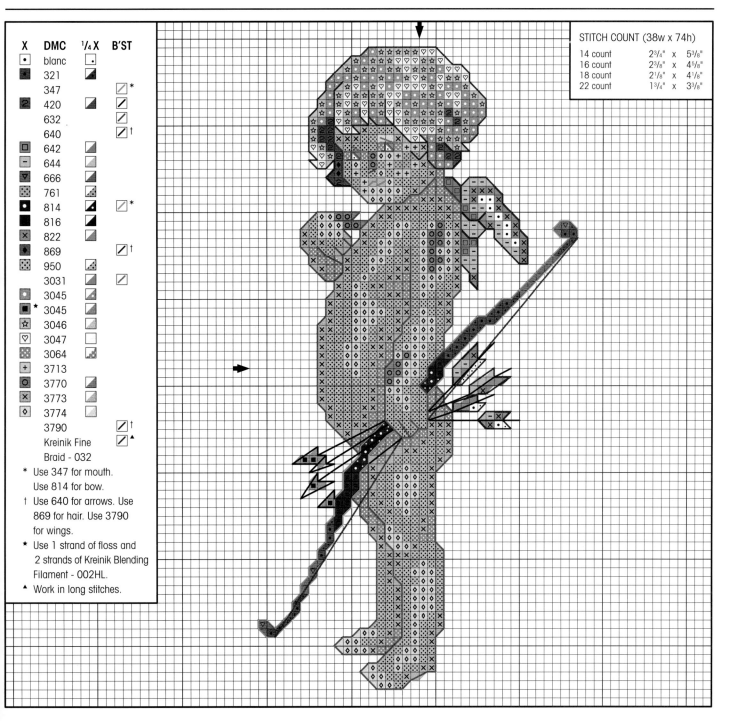

X	DMC	¼ X	B'ST
•	blanc	•	
✦	321	◪	
	347		◹ *
2	420	◪	◹
	632		◹
	640		◹ †
▢	642	◩	
−	644	◩	
▽	666	◪	
∴	761	◪	
◼	814	◪	◹ *
■	816	◪	
✕	822	◪	
◆	869	◪	◹ †
⁚⁚	950	◩	
	3031	◪	◹
▢	3045	◪	
■ ★	3045		
☆	3046	◩	
♡	3047	▢	
▦	3064	◪	
+	3713		
○	3770	◪	
✕	3773	◩	
◇	3774	◩	
	3790		◹ †
	Kreinik Fine		◹ ▲
	Braid - 032		

* Use 347 for mouth.
  Use 814 for bow.
† Use 640 for arrows. Use
  869 for hair. Use 3790
  for wings.
★ Use 1 strand of floss and
  2 strands of Kreinik Blending
  Filament - 002HL.
▲ Work in long stitches.

STITCH COUNT (38w x 74h)

14 count	2³/₄"	x	5³/₈"
16 count	2³/₈"	x	4⁵/₈"
18 count	2¹/₈"	x	4¹/₈"
22 count	1³/₄"	x	3³/₈"

Cherub Wreath (shown on page 6): The design was stitched over 2 fabric threads on an 11" x 13" piece of Antique White Cashel Linen® (28 ct). Three strands of floss were used for Cross Stitch and 1 strand for Backstitch. It was custom framed and attached to a 17" dia. decorated wreath.

Cherub Pillow (shown on page 8): The design was stitched over 2 fabric threads on an 11" x 19" piece of Antique White Cashel Linen® (28 ct). Three strands of floss were used for Cross Stitch and 1 strand for Backstitch.

For pillow, you will need two 17" lengths of ³/₄"w flat lace, two 17" lengths of ¹/₈"w gold trim, two 10¹/₂" x 13" pieces of fabric for pillow front and back, and polyester fiberfill.

Centering design, trim stitched piece to measure 9¹/₂" x 17".

For band, fold stitched piece in half matching right sides and long edges.

Using a ¹/₂" seam allowance, sew long edges together; turn stitched piece right side out. With seam centered in back, press stitched piece flat. Referring to photo for placement, blind stitch lace and gold trim to each long edge of band. Matching right side and short edges, use a ¹/₂" seam allowance to sew short edges together; press seam open and turn band right side out.

For pillow, match right sides and raw edges of pillow front and back. Leaving an opening for turning, use a ¹/₂" seam allowance to sew fabric pieces together; trim seam allowances diagonally at corners. Turn pillow right side out, carefully pushing corners outward; stuff pillow lightly with polyester fiberfill and blind stitch opening closed.

Referring to photo, place band around pillow.

Needlework adaptation by Donna Vermillion Giampa.

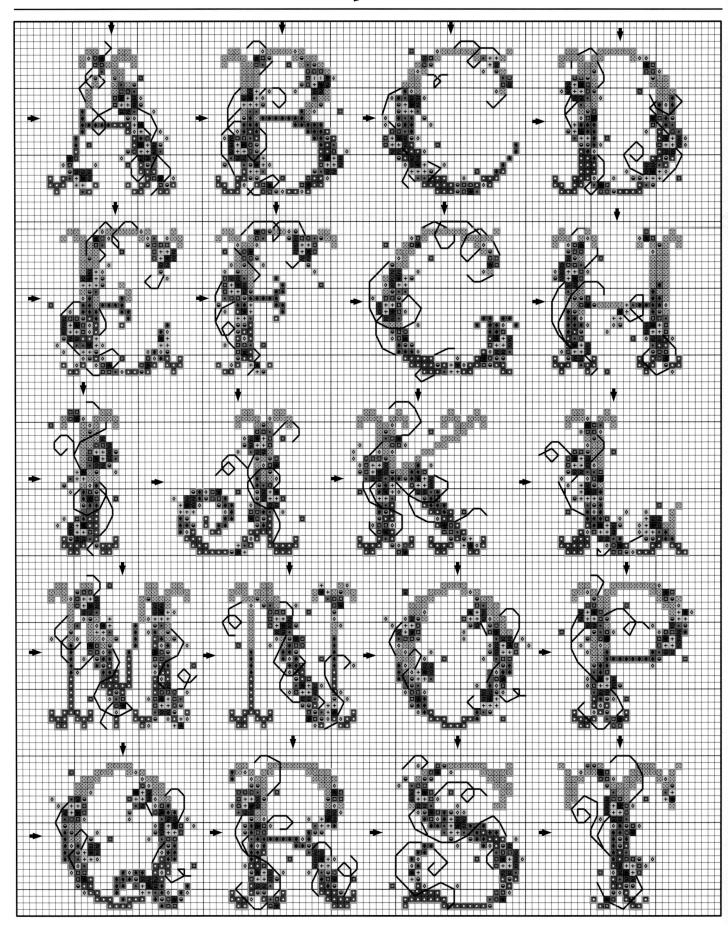

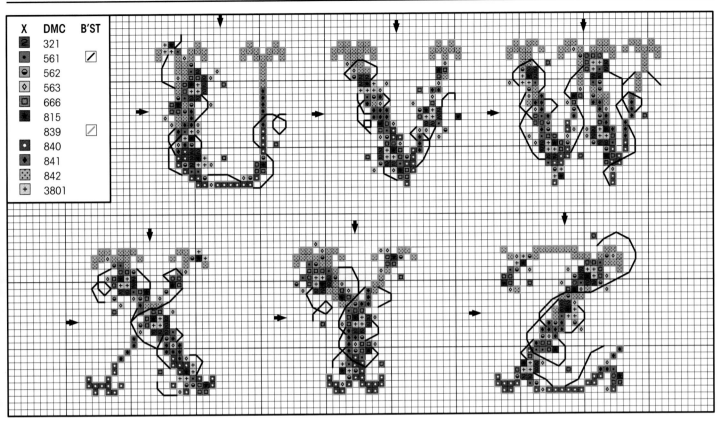

X	DMC	B'ST
▨	321	
●	561	╱
◖	562	
◇	563	
▢	666	
✴	815	
	839	╱
▣	840	
◆	841	
▦	842	
✚	3801	

Floral Monogram Sachet Bag (shown on page 9): The letter "W" was stitched over 2 fabric threads on an 8" x 10" piece of Antique White Belfast Linen (32 ct). Two strands of floss were used for Cross Stitch and 1 strand for Backstitch.

For sachet bag, you will need a 4" x 6½" piece of Belfast Linen for backing, 7" length of ¾"w flat lace, 7" length of ⅛"w gold trim, 21" length of ⅝"w ribbon, polyester fiberfill, and scented oil.

Trim stitched piece to measure 4" x 6½", allowing 1¼" margins at sides and bottom of design and a 4" margin at top of design.

Matching right sides and leaving top edge open, use a ½" seam allowance to sew stitched piece and backing fabric together; trim seam allowances diagonally at corners. Turn top edge of bag ¼" to wrong side and press; turn ¼" to wrong side again and hem. Press short edges of lace ½" to wrong side. Blind stitch straight edge of lace to wrong side of top edge of bag; turn bag right side out. Referring to photo, blind stitch gold trim to top edge of bag; stuff bag with polyester fiberfill. Place a few drops of scented oil on a small amount of fiberfill and insert in bag. Tie ribbon in a bow around bag; trim ends as desired.

Floral Monogram Jar Lid (shown on page 9): The letter "R" was stitched over 2 fabric threads on a 6" square of Antique White Belfast Linen (32 ct). Two strands of floss were used for Cross Stitch and 1 strand for Backstitch. It was inserted in the lid of a round gold jar (2⅝" dia. opening).

Floral Monogram Towel (shown on page 9): The letters "K", "S", and "M" were stitched over 2 fabric threads across one short end of a 12" x 20" piece of Antique White Belfast Linen (32 ct) with 4 stitches between each letter. Center design horizontally with bottom of design 2" from short edge. Two strands of floss were used for Cross Stitch and 1 strand for Backstitch.

For each towel, you will need a 12" length of ¾"w flat lace and a 12" length of ⅛"w gold trim.

On each short edge, turn fabric ¼" to wrong side and press; turn ¼" to wrong side again and hem. Referring to photo, blind stitch lace and gold trim to right side of towel on cross stitched end. For remaining raw edges, turn fabric ¼" to wrong side and press; turn ¼" to wrong side again and hem.

Floral Monogram Sachet Pillow (shown on page 9): The letter "G" was stitched over 2 fabric threads on an 8" square of Antique White Belfast Linen (32 ct). Two strands of floss were used for Cross Stitch and 1 strand for Backstitch.

For pillow, you will need a 4" square of Belfast Linen for backing, 15" length of ¾"w flat lace, 15" length of ⅛"w gold trim, polyester fiberfill, and scented oil.

Centering design, trim stitched piece to measure 4" square.

Matching right sides and leaving an opening for turning, use a ¼" seam allowance to sew stitched piece and backing fabric together. Trim seam allowances diagonally at corners; turn sachet right side out, carefully pushing corners outward. Stuff sachet with polyester fiberfill; place a few drops of scented oil on a small amount of polyester fiberfill and insert in sachet. Blind stitch opening closed.

Press short edges of lace and gold trim ½" to wrong side. Beginning and ending at bottom center of pillow, blind stitch lace to edges of pillow. Referring to photo for placement, repeat for gold trim.

"Love" Bookmark (shown on page 9): The word "LOVE" was stitched over 2 fabric threads on a 6" x 11" piece of Antique White Belfast Linen (32 ct). Center letters horizontally with 4 stitches between each letter. Two strands of floss were used for Cross Stitch and 1 strand for Backstitch.

For bookmark, you will need two 3¼" lengths of ¾"w flat lace and two 3¼" lengths of ⅛"w gold trim.

Centering design, trim stitched piece to measure 3¼" x 8".

On one long edge, turn fabric ¼" to wrong side and press; turn ¼" to wrong side again and hem. Repeat for remaining long edge. For remaining raw edges, turn fabric ¼" to wrong side and press; turn ¼" to wrong side again and hem. Referring to photo for placement, blind stitch lace and gold trim to each short edge. Turn raw edges to wrong side of bookmark and tack in place.

Designs by Diane Brakefield.

STITCH COUNT (110w x 90h)

count	width	x	height
14 count	7⁷⁄₈"	x	6¹⁄₂"
16 count	6⁷⁄₈"	x	5⁵⁄₈"
18 count	6¹⁄₈"	x	5"
22 count	5"	x	4¹⁄₈"

May your neighbors respect you, Trouble neglect you, The angels protect you, And Heaven accept you,

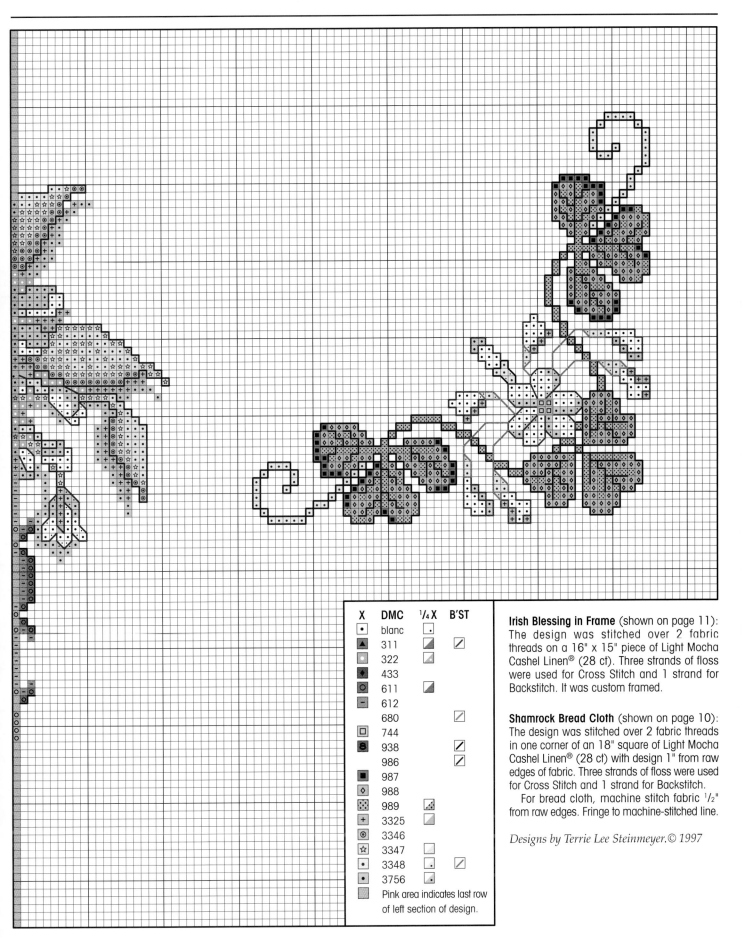

X	DMC	¼ X	B'ST
•	blanc	•	
▲	311	◤	╱
◐	322	◢	
◆	433	◤	
◉	611	◢	
-	612		
	680		╱
□	744		
▨	938		╱
	986		╱
■	987		
◇	988		
▨	989	◢	
+	3325	◢	
◉	3346		
☆	3347	◹	
•	3348	•	╱
•	3756	◢	
▨	Pink area indicates last row of left section of design.		

Irish Blessing in Frame (shown on page 11): The design was stitched over 2 fabric threads on a 16" x 15" piece of Light Mocha Cashel Linen® (28 ct). Three strands of floss were used for Cross Stitch and 1 strand for Backstitch. It was custom framed.

Shamrock Bread Cloth (shown on page 10): The design was stitched over 2 fabric threads in one corner of an 18" square of Light Mocha Cashel Linen® (28 ct) with design 1" from raw edges of fabric. Three strands of floss were used for Cross Stitch and 1 strand for Backstitch.

For bread cloth, machine stitch fabric ½" from raw edges. Fringe to machine-stitched line.

Designs by Terrie Lee Steinmeyer.© 1997

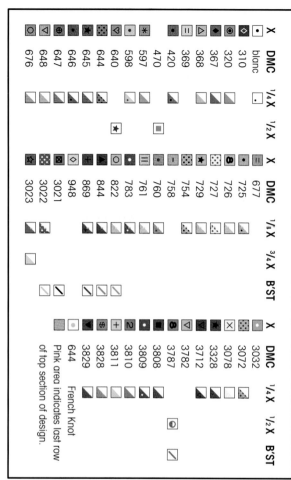

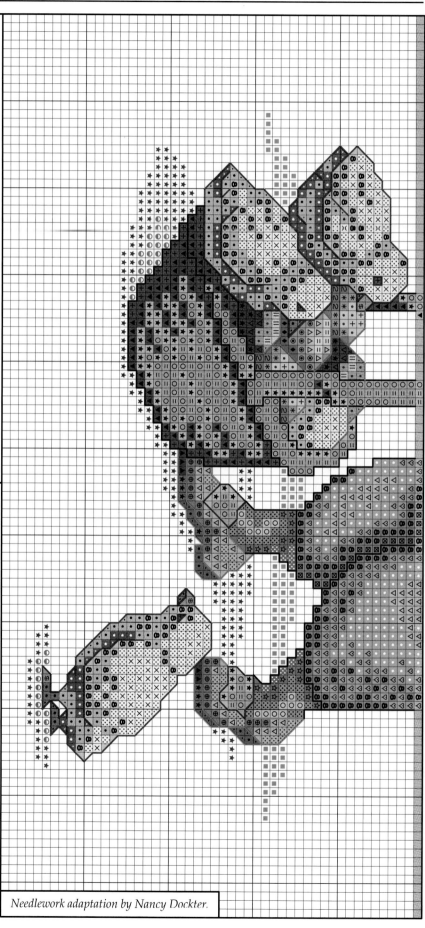

Easter Visitor in Frame (shown on page 14): The design was stitched on a 15" x 17" piece of Antique White Aida (14 ct). Three strands of floss were used for Cross Stitch and 1 strand for Half Cross Stitch, Backstitch, and French Knots. It was custom framed.

Easter Visitor Afghan (shown on page 13): The design was stitched over 2 fabric threads on a 45" x 58" piece of Soft White All-Cotton Anne Cloth (18 ct).

For afghan, cut selvages from fabric; measure 8" from raw edge of fabric and pull out 1 fabric thread. Fringe fabric up to missing fabric thread. Repeat for each side. Tie an overhand knot at each corner with 4 horizontal and 4 vertical fabric threads. Working from corners, use 8 fabric threads for each knot until all threads are knotted.

Refer to Diagram for placement of design on fabric; use 6 strands of floss for Cross Stitch and 2 strands for Half Cross Stitch, Backstitch, and French Knots.

Diagram

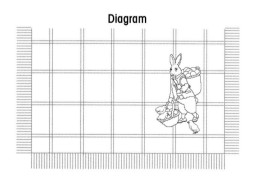

Needlework adaptation by Nancy Dockter.

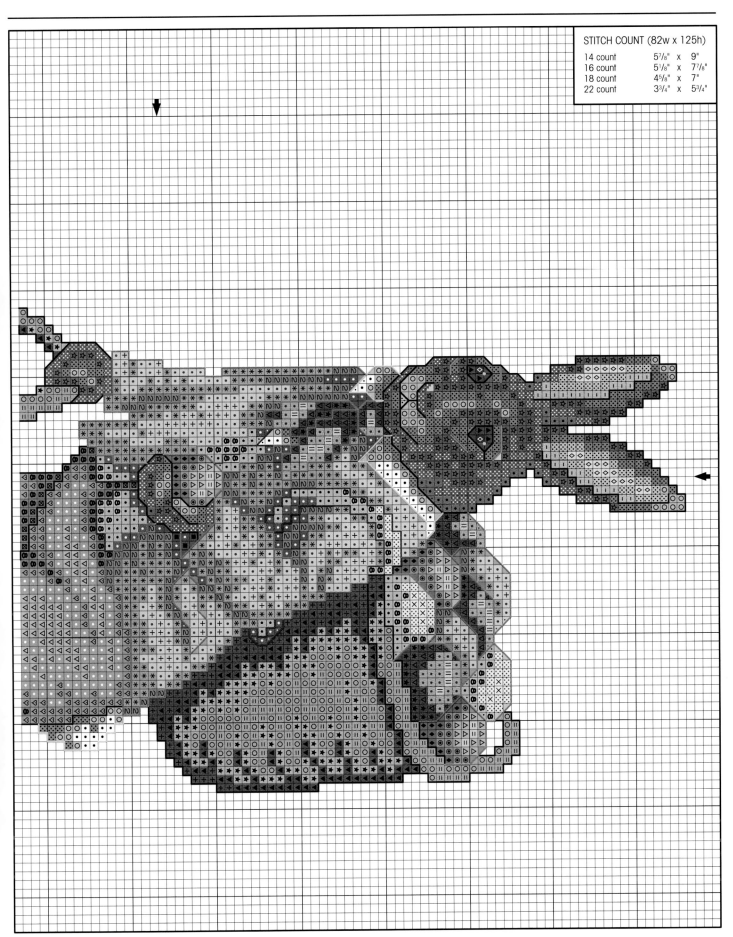

STITCH COUNT (82w x 125h)

14 count	5⁷⁄₈"	x	9"
16 count	5¹⁄₈"	x	7⁷⁄₈"
18 count	4⁵⁄₈"	x	7"
22 count	3³⁄₄"	x	5³⁄₄"

EASTER

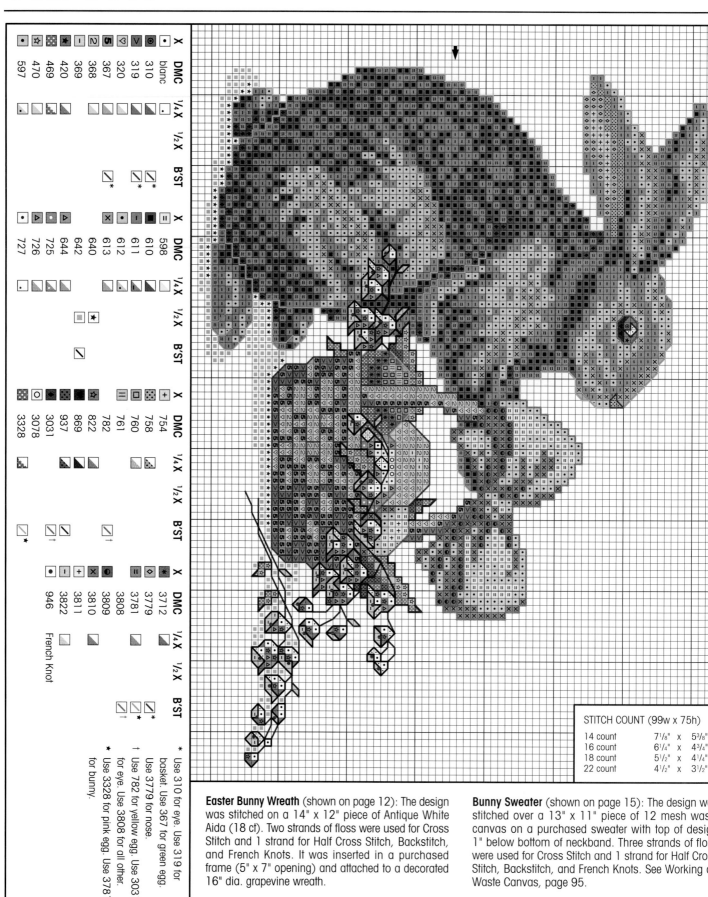

STITCH COUNT (99w x 75h)

14 count	7⅛"	x 5⅜"
16 count	6¼"	x 4¾"
18 count	5½"	x 4¼"
22 count	4½"	x 3½"

Easter Bunny Wreath (shown on page 12): The design was stitched on a 14" x 12" piece of Antique White Aida (18 ct). Two strands of floss were used for Cross Stitch and 1 strand for Half Cross Stitch, Backstitch, and French Knots. It was inserted in a purchased frame (5" x 7" opening) and attached to a decorated 16" dia. grapevine wreath.

Bunny Sweater (shown on page 15): The design was stitched over a 13" x 11" piece of 12 mesh waste canvas on a purchased sweater with top of design 1" below bottom of neckband. Three strands of floss were used for Cross Stitch and 1 strand for Half Cross Stitch, Backstitch, and French Knots. See Working on Waste Canvas, page 95.

Needlework adaptation by Nancy Dockter.

* Use 310 for eye. Use 319 for basket. Use 367 for green egg. Use 3779 for nose.
† Use 782 for yellow egg. Use 3031 for eye. Use 3808 for all other.
* Use 3328 for pink egg. Use 3781 for bunny.

58

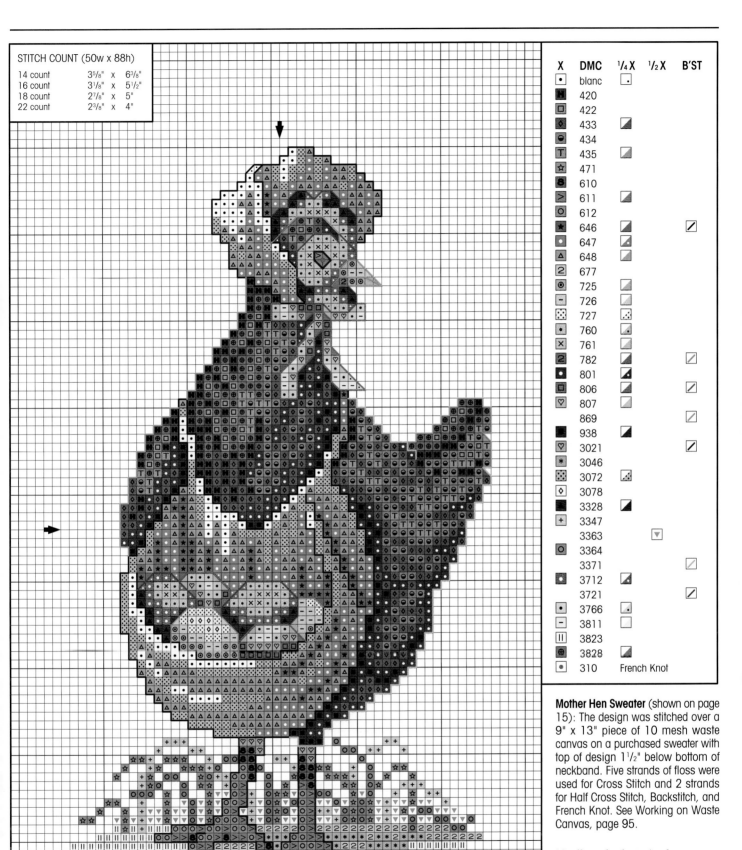

STITCH COUNT (50w x 88h)

14 count	3⅝" x	6⅜"
16 count	3⅛" x	5½"
18 count	2⅞" x	5"
22 count	2⅜" x	4"

X	DMC	¼ X	½ X	B'ST
•	blanc	•		
⋈	420			
□	422			
◇	433	◢		
⊖	434			
T	435	◢		
☆	471			
8	610			
>	611	◢		
O	612			
★	646	◢		◹
⊙	647	◢		
△	648	◢		
2	677			
⊙	725	◢		
–	726		◢	
⠿	727	⠿		
•	760	•		
X	761	◢		
2	782	◢		◹
●	801	◢		
□	806	◢		◹
♡	807	□		
	869			◹
▩	938	◢		
▽	3021			
*	3046			
⠿	3072	⠿		
◇	3078			
■	3328	◢		
+	3347			
	3363		▽	
O	3364			
	3371			◹
▣	3712	◢		
	3721			◹
•	3766	•		
–	3811	□		
‖	3823			
⊕	3828	◢		
⊙	310	French Knot		

Mother Hen Sweater (shown on page 15): The design was stitched over a 9" x 13" piece of 10 mesh waste canvas on a purchased sweater with top of design 1½" below bottom of neckband. Five strands of floss were used for Cross Stitch and 2 strands for Half Cross Stitch, Backstitch, and French Knot. See Working on Waste Canvas, page 95.

Needlework adaptation by Nancy Dockter.

59

EASTER

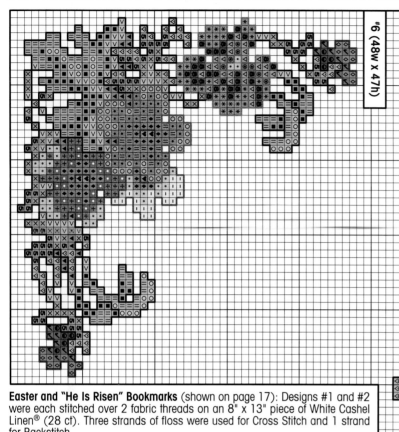

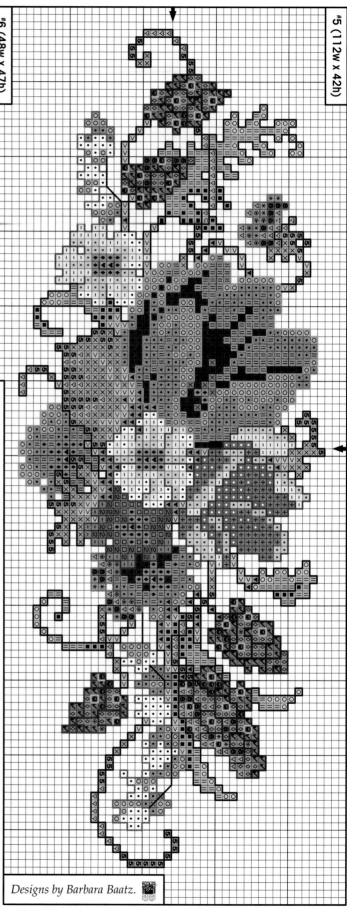

#6 (48w x 47h)

#5 (112w x 42h)

Easter and "He Is Risen" Bookmarks (shown on page 17): Designs #1 and #2 were each stitched over 2 fabric threads on an 8" x 13" piece of White Cashel Linen® (28 ct). Three strands of floss were used for Cross Stitch and 1 strand for Backstitch.

For each bookmark, you will need two 4" lengths of ¹/₂"w lace, a 12" length of ⁷/₈"w ribbon, and fabric glue.

Centering design, trim stitched piece to measure 4" x 8".

On one long edge, turn fabric ¹/₄" to wrong side and press; turn ¹/₄" to wrong side again and hem. Repeat for remaining long edge. For remaining raw edges, turn fabric ¹/₄" to wrong side and press; turn ¹/₄" to wrong side again and hem. Blind stitch lace to each short edge. Turn raw edges of lace to wrong side and blind stitch in place.

Referring to photo for placement, glue right side of ribbon to wrong side of stitched piece. Trim ends as desired.

Spring Floral Shirt (shown on page 17): Design #3 was stitched over a 3" square piece of 14 mesh waste canvas on the collar of a purchased shirt. Three strands of floss were used for Cross Stitch and 1 strand for Backstitch. See Working on Waste Canvas, page 95.

Spring Floral Bread Cloth (shown on page 16): Design #6 was stitched over 2 fabric threads in one corner of a 19" square of White Cashel Linen® (28 ct) with design 1" from raw edges of fabric. Three strands of floss were used for Cross Stitch and 1 strand for Backstitch.

For bread cloth, you will need a 75" length of ¹/₂"w lace. Press short edges of lace ¹/₂" to wrong side. Turn each edge of stitched piece ¹/₄" to wrong side and press; turn ¹/₄" to wrong side again and hem. Referring to photo, blind stitch straight edge of lace to wrong side of bread cloth.

Spring Floral Table Runner (shown on page 16): Design #5 was stitched over 2 fabric threads across each short end of a 16" x 40" piece of White Cashel Linen® (28 ct) with bottom of design 4" from raw edge of fabric. Three strands of floss were used for Cross Stitch and 1 strand for Backstitch.

For table runner, you will need two 16" lengths of 2"w lace and two 1" x 16" bias fabric strips.

For trim, fold fabric strip in half lengthwise with wrong sides together; press. Matching raw edges of fabric strip to straight edge of lace; baste together. Repeat for remaining fabric strip and lace.

On cross-stitched ends, match right sides and straight edges of trim to raw edge of fabric and use a ¹/₄" seam allowance to sew trim to right side of fabric. Using a zigzag stitch to prevent fraying, sew close to seam; trim close to zigzag stitch. Press seam allowance to wrong side of table runner. For remaining raw edges, turn fabric ¹/₄" to wrong side and press; turn ¹/₄" to wrong side again and hem.

Designs by Barbara Baatz.

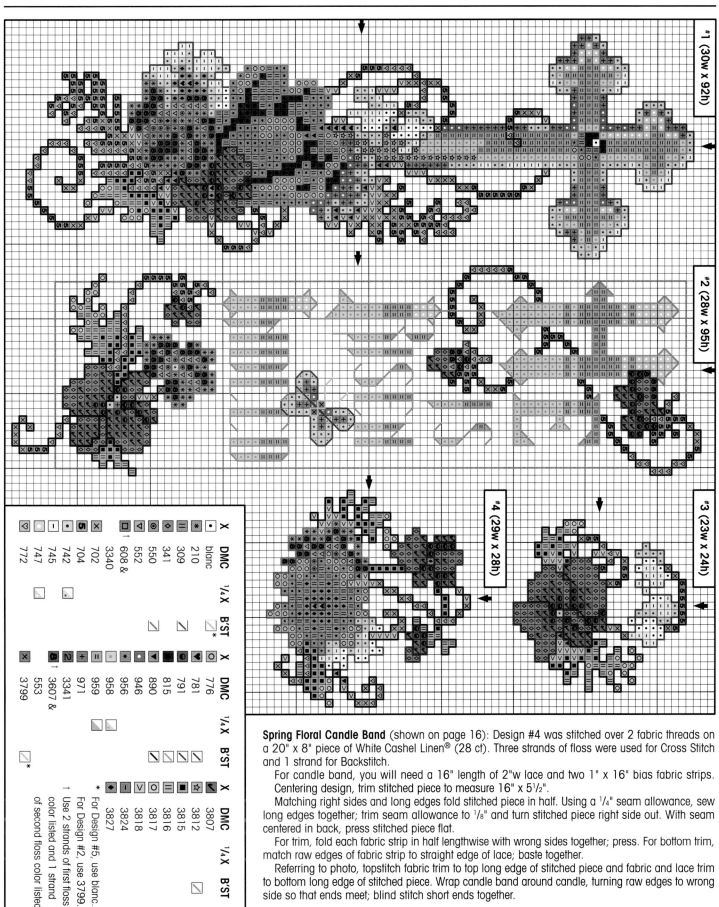

Spring Floral Candle Band (shown on page 16): Design #4 was stitched over 2 fabric threads on a 20" x 8" piece of White Cashel Linen® (28 ct). Three strands of floss were used for Cross Stitch and 1 strand for Backstitch.

For candle band, you will need a 16" length of 2"w lace and two 1" x 16" bias fabric strips. Centering design, trim stitched piece to measure 16" x 5½".

Matching right sides and long edges fold stitched piece in half. Using a ¼" seam allowance, sew long edges together; trim seam allowance to ⅛" and turn stitched piece right side out. With seam centered in back, press stitched piece flat.

For trim, fold each fabric strip in half lengthwise with wrong sides together; press. For bottom trim, match raw edges of fabric strip to straight edge of lace; baste together.

Referring to photo, topstitch fabric trim to top long edge of stitched piece and fabric and lace trim to bottom long edge of stitched piece. Wrap candle band around candle, turning raw edges to wrong side so that ends meet; blind stitch short ends together.

X	DMC	¼ X	B'ST
▼	610	◹	◹
▣	611	◹	
▢	612	◹	
✕	613	◹	
✚	644	◹	
☆	772	◹	
•	819	◹	
	935		◹
★	961	◹	
═	962	◹	
△	963	◹	
■	3345	◹	◹
◨	3346	◹	◹
◎	3347	◹	
–	3348	◹	
	3350		◹
▦	3716	◹	
•	610	French Knot	
•*	725	French Knot	
•	3346	French Knot	
▢	Blue area indicates last row of left section of design.		

* Use 2 strands of floss.

STITCH COUNT (148w x 108h)

14 count	10⅝"	x	7¾"	
16 count	9¼"	x	6¾"	
18 count	8¼"	x	6"	
22 count	6¾"	x	5"	

"The Old Rugged Cross" in Frame (shown on page 18): The design was stitched over 2 fabric threads on a 19" x 16" piece of Platinum Cashel Linen® (28 ct). Three strands of floss were used for Cross Stitch and 1 strand for Backstitch and French Knots, unless otherwise noted in the color key. It was custom framed.

Design by Donna Vermillion Giampa.

INDEPENDENCE DAY

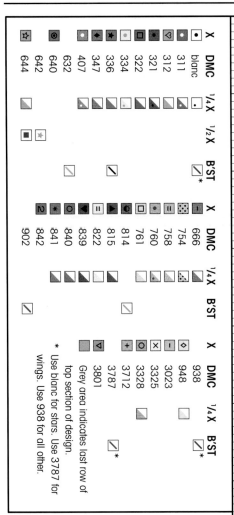

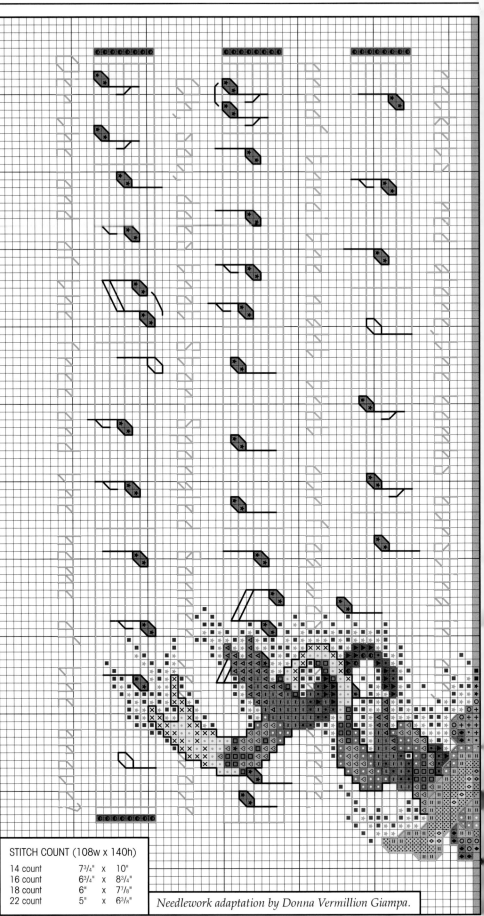

X	DMC	¼X	½X	B'ST
✓	blanc	✓		✓*
✓	311	✓		
✓	312	✓		
✓	321	✓		
✓	322	✓		
✓	334	✓		
✓	336	✓		✓
✓	347	✓		
✓	407	✓		
	632			✓
✓	640			
	642		✓	
✓	644	✓	✓	

X	DMC	¼X	B'ST
✓	666	✓	
✓	754	✓	
✓	758	✓	
✓	760	✓	
✓	761	✓	
✓	814		✓
✓	815	✓	
✓	822	✓	
✓	839	✓	
✓	840	✓	
✓	841	✓	
✓	842		
	902		✓

X	DMC	¼X	B'ST
✓	938		✓*
✓	948	✓	
✓	3023		
✓	3325		
✓	3328	✓	
✓	3712		
	3787		✓*
✓	3801		

Grey area indicates last row of top section of design.

* Use blanc for stars. Use 3787 for wings. Use 938 for all other.

STITCH COUNT (108w x 140h)			
14 count	7¾"	x	10"
16 count	6¾"	x	8¾"
18 count	6"	x	7⅞"
22 count	5"	x	6⅜"

Needlework adaptation by Donna Vermillion Giampa.

"The Star-Spangled Banner" in Frame (shown on page 21): The design was stitched over 2 fabric threads on a 17" x 19" piece of Pewter Lugana (25 ct). Three strands of floss were used for Cross Stitch and 1 strand for Half Cross Stitch and Backstitch. It was custom framed.

Liberty Angel Bookmark (shown on page 20): The angel only from "The Star-Spangled Banner" design (refer to photo) was stitched on a 7" x 9" piece of Ivory Aida (14 ct). Three strands of floss were used for Cross Stitch and 1 strand for Backstitch.

For bookmark, you will need a 7" x 9" piece of lightweight cream fabric for backing, fabric stiffener, small foam brush, 7" length of 1½"w ribbon, and clear-drying craft glue. Apply a heavy coat of fabric stiffener to back of stitched piece using small foam brush. Matching wrong sides, place stitched piece on backing fabric, smoothing stitched piece while pressing fabric pieces together; allow to dry. Apply fabric stiffener to backing fabric; allow to dry. Cut out close to edges of stitched design. Referring to photo, glue wrong side of stiffened angel to ribbon. Trim end of ribbon as desired.

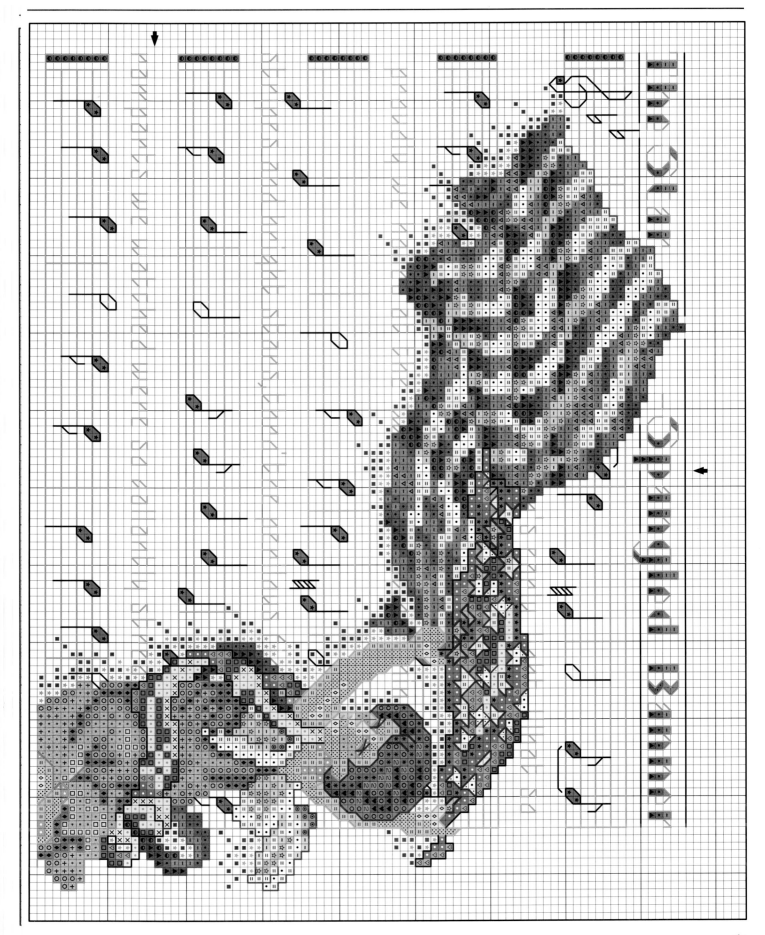

Thanksgiving

center date

center initials

Harvest Sampler in Frame (shown on page 33): The design was stitched over 2 fabric threads on a 14" x 19" piece of Raw Belfast Linen (32 ct). Two strands of DMC 924 floss were used for Cross Stitch and 1 strand for Backstitch. Personalize and date sampler with DMC 924 floss using alphabet and numerals from chart. It was custom framed.

Harvest Table Runner (shown on page 34): A portion of the Harvest Sampler (refer to photo) was stitched over 2 fabric threads across each short end of a 16" x 40" piece of Cream Cashel Linen® (28 ct) with bottom of design 2" from raw edge of fabric. Three strands of DMC 920 floss were used for Cross Stitch.

For table runner, machine stitch across each short edge of fabric 1/2" from

raw edges. Fringe to machine-stitched line. On one long edge, turn fabric 1/4" to wrong side and press; turn 1/4" to wrong side again and hem. Repeat for remaining long edge.

Harvest Bread Cloth (shown on page 34): A portion of the border of the Harvest Sampler (refer to photo) was stitched over 2 fabric threads in one corner of a 20" square of Cream Cashel Linen® (28 ct) with design 1" from raw edges of fabric. Three strands of DMC 920 floss were used for Cross Stitch.

For bread cloth, machine stitch around fabric 1/2" from raw edges. Fringe to machine-stitched line.

Harvest Napkin Ring (shown on page 34): A portion of the Harvest Sampler (refer to photo) was stitched over 2 fabric threads on a 6" x 12" piece of Cream Cashel Linen® (28 ct). Three strands of DMC 920 floss were used for Cross Stitch.

Centering design, trim stitched piece to measure 7¹/₂" x 4³/₄".

Matching right sides and long edges, fold stitched piece in half. Use ¹/₄" seam allowance to sew long edges together. Trim seam allowance to ¹/₈" and turn stitched piece right side out. With seam centered in back, press stitched piece flat. Press short edges ¹/₂" to wrong side. Blind stitch short edges together.

Design by Deborah Lambein.

STITCH COUNT (89w x 177h)		
14 count	6³/₈" x	12³/₄"
16 count	5⁵/₈" x	11¹/₈"
18 count	5" x	9⁷/₈"
22 count	4¹/₈" x	8¹/₈"

thanksgiving

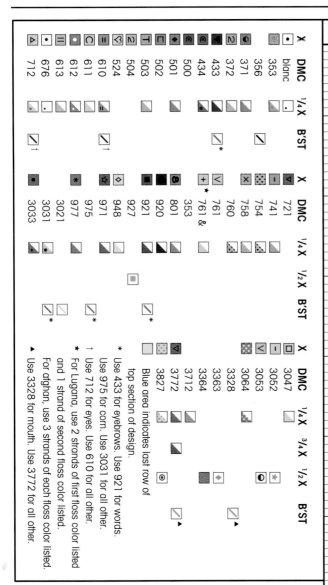

Needlework adaptation by Nancy Dockter.

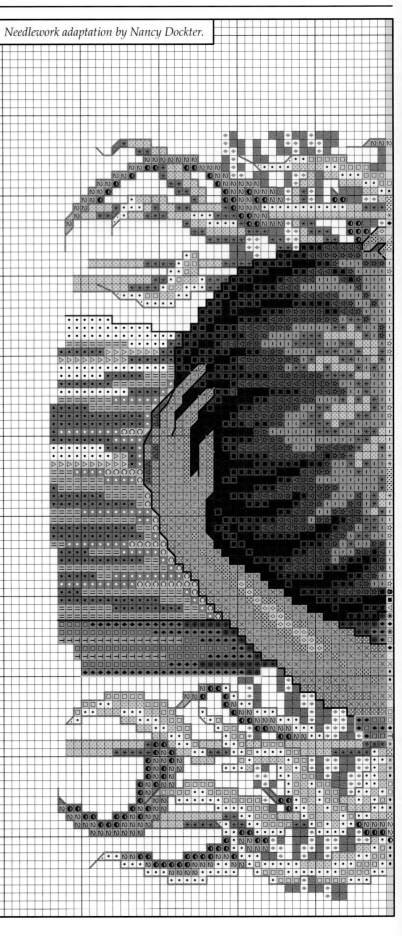

Harvesttime in Frame (shown on page 35): The design was stitched over 2 fabric threads on a 16" x 18" piece of Cream Lugana (25 ct). Three strands of floss were used for Cross Stitch and 1 strand for Half Cross Stitch and Backstitch. It was custom framed.

Harvesttime Afghan (shown on page 37): A portion of the Harvesttime design (refer to photo) was stitched over 2 fabric threads on a 45" x 58" piece of Ivory All-Cotton Anne Cloth (18 ct).

For afghan, cut selvages from fabric. Machine stitch along raised threads around outside edge of afghan. Fringe fabric to machine-stitched lines.

Refer to Diagram for placement of design on fabric. Six strands of floss were used for Cross Stitch and 2 strands for Backstitch.

DIAGRAM

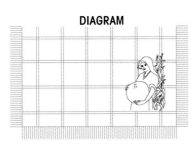

STITCH COUNT (96w x 128h)

14 count	6⅞" x	9¼"
16 count	6" x	8"
18 count	5⅜" x	7⅛"
22 count	4⅜" x	5⅞"

thanksgiving

42w x 54h

X	DMC	¼ X	B'ST		X	DMC	¼ X	B'ST
	310		◢*			920		◿
●	433	◢			◆	921	◢	
▨	434	◢				936		◢*
=	436	◢			●	937	◢	
+	469	◢			●	971	◢	
○	470				✕	3021	◢	
▨	721	◢			▲	3325	◢	
☆	741				●	3755	◢	
□	742	◢			-	3756		
●	801	◢						

* Use 310 for writing.
Use 936 for all other.

Pumpkin Seed Packet in Frame (shown on page 34): The design was stitched over 2 fabric threads on an 11" x 12" piece of Cream Cashel Linen® (28 ct). Three strands of floss were used for Cross Stitch and 1 strand for Backstitch. It was custom framed.

Pumpkin Seed Packet Shirt (shown on page 39): The design was stitched over a 6" x 7" piece of 14 mesh waste canvas on the pocket of a purchased chambray shirt. Center design horizontally with top of design approximately ¾" below top edge of pocket. Three strands of floss were used for Cross Stitch and 1 strand for Backstitch. See Working on Waste Canvas, page 95.

Design by Nancy Dockter.

St. Nick Sweater (shown on page 47, chart on page 85): The design was stitched over a 12" x 10" piece of 12 mesh waste canvas on a purchased sweater with top of design ¾" below bottom of neckband. Three strands of floss were used for Cross Stitch and 1 strand of floss or braid for Half Cross Stitch and Backstitch. See Working on Waste Canvas, page 95.

St. Nick Wall Hanging (shown on page 46, chart on page 85): The design was stitched over 2 fabric threads on a 19" square of Antique White Aida (16 ct). Six strands of floss were used for Cross Stitch and 2 strands of floss or braid for Half Cross Stitch and Backstitch.

For wall hanging, you will need ¼ yd total of assorted fabrics for pieced borders, ¾ yd piece of fabric for outer borders and backing, 18¼" square piece of batting, and 3" x 17¼" fabric strip for hanging sleeve.

Centering design, trim stitched piece to measure 13" square.

For pieced fabric borders, cut twenty-eight 3" square pieces from assorted fabrics.

Note: When piecing wall hanging, always match right sides and raw edges. Use ½" seam allowance for all seams.

Using 6 squares for each top and bottom border and 8 squares for each

side border, sew squares together. Press seams to one side. Sew one long edge of top border to top of stitched piece; repeat for bottom border. Press seams toward borders. Sew one long edge of one side border to each side of stitched piece and top and bottom borders. Press seams toward borders.

For outer borders, cut two 1⅝" x 17" fabric strips for top and bottom borders and two 1⅝" x 18¼" fabric strips for side borders. Sew one long edge of top outer border to top of wall hanging; repeat for bottom outer border. Sew one long edge of one outer side border to each side of wall hanging and top and bottom outer borders.

For backing, cut a piece of fabric same size as wall hanging front.

Matching right sides and raw edges, place backing fabric on wall hanging front; place batting on backing fabric. Sew all three layers together, leaving an opening for turning. Trim corners diagonally and turn right side out. Blind stitch opening closed.

For hanging sleeve, press all edges ¼" to wrong side and machine stitch pressed edges in place. With one long edge of hanging sleeve ¼" below top of wall hanging, center and pin hanging sleeve to backing. Whipstitch long edges of hanging sleeve to backing.

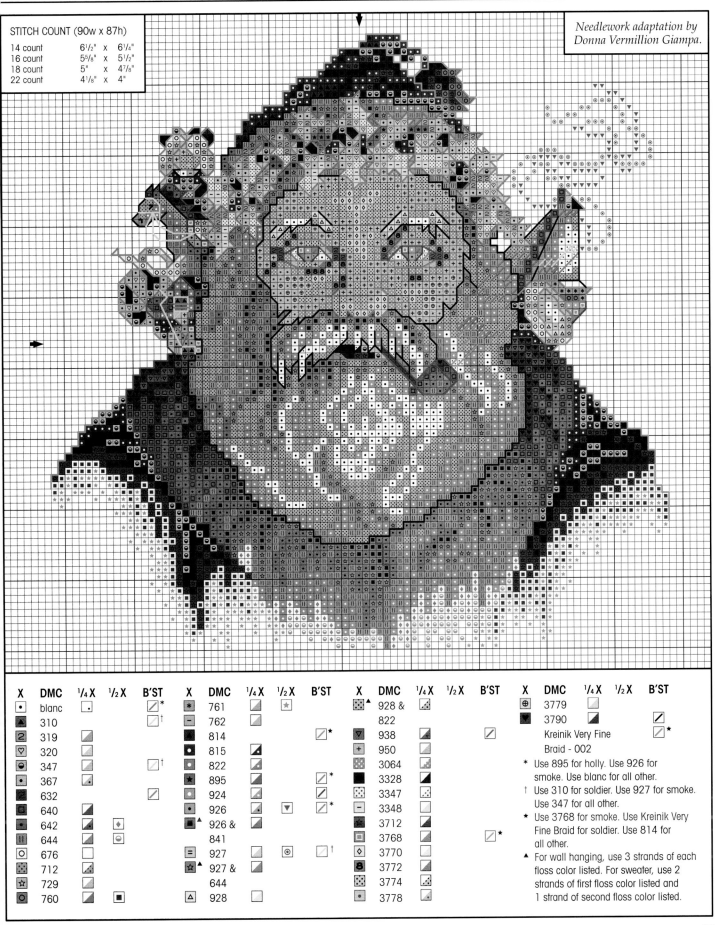

STITCH COUNT (90w x 87h)

14 count	6½"	x	6¼"
16 count	5⅝"	x	5½"
18 count	5"	x	4⅞"
22 count	4⅛"	x	4"

Needlework adaptation by Donna Vermillion Giampa.

X	DMC	¼ X	½ X	B'ST	X	DMC	¼ X	½ X	B'ST	X	DMC	¼ X	½ X	B'ST	X	DMC	¼ X	½ X	B'ST
•	blanc			*	*	761			★		928 &				⊕	3779			
	310			†	—	762					822				▼	3790			
2	319					814			*	▼	938					Kreinik Very Fine			*
♥	320					815				+	950					Braid - 002			
◉	347			†		822					3064								
•	367				★	895			*		3328								
2	632					924					3347								
	640				•	926		▼	*	—	3348								
•	642		♦			926 &				★	3712								
‖	644					841					3768			*					
○	676				=	927		⊙	†	♦	3770								
	712				★	927 &				8	3772								
☆	729					644					3774								
◎	760				△	928				•	3778								

* Use 895 for holly. Use 926 for smoke. Use blanc for all other.

† Use 310 for soldier. Use 927 for smoke. Use 347 for all other.

★ Use 3768 for smoke. Use Kreinik Very Fine Braid for soldier. Use 814 for all other.

▲ For wall hanging, use 3 strands of each floss color listed. For sweater, use 2 strands of first floss color listed and 1 strand of second floss color listed.

CHRISTMAS

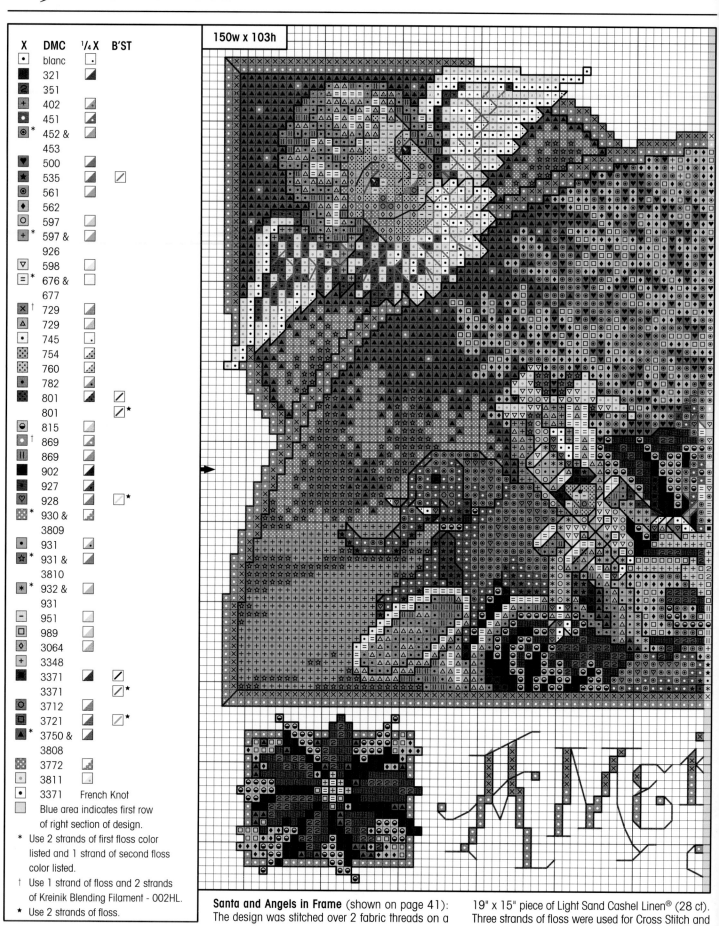

X	DMC	¼ X	B'ST
•	blanc		
■	321		
2	351		
+	402		
■	451		
⊙ *	452 &		
	453		
▼	500		
★	535		╱
⊙	561		
◆	562		
○	597		
+ *	597 &		
	926		
▽	598		
= *	676 &		
	677		
✕ †	729		
△	729		
•	745		
▦	754		
▦	760		
▪	782		
▨	801		╱
	801		╱*
◖	815		
◖ †	869		
‖	869		
■	902		
▩	927		
♡	928		╱*
▨ *	930 &		
	3809		
•	931		
☆ *	931 &		
	3810		
✳ *	932 &		
	931		
−	951		
□	989		
◇	3064		
+	3348		
■	3371		╱
	3371		╱*
◎	3712		
▣	3721		╱*
▲ *	3750 &		
	3808		
▨	3772		
◦	3811		
•	3371	French Knot	

Blue area indicates first row of right section of design.

* Use 2 strands of first floss color listed and 1 strand of second floss color listed.

† Use 1 strand of floss and 2 strands of Kreinik Blending Filament - 002HL.

* Use 2 strands of floss.

150w x 103h

Santa and Angels in Frame (shown on page 41):
The design was stitched over 2 fabric threads on a

19" x 15" piece of Light Sand Cashel Linen® (28 ct).
Three strands of floss were used for Cross Stitch and

1 strand for Backstitch and French Knot, unless otherwise noted in the color key. It was custom framed.

Needlework adapatation by Sandy Orton.

CHRISTMAS

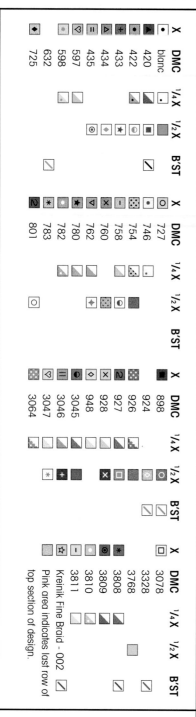

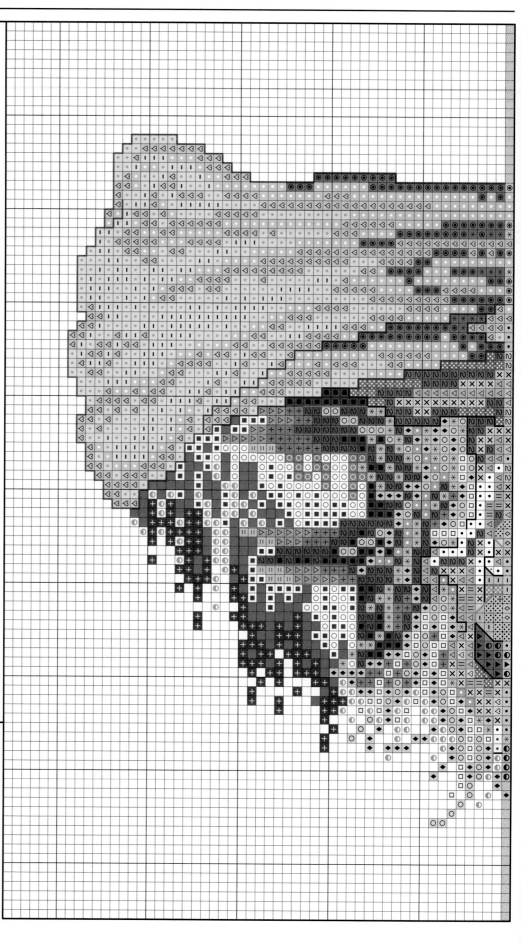

X	◆		◁	‖	▷	✛	●	▶	·	X
DMC		·	◁	‖	▷	✛	●	▶	·	blanc
725	632	598	597	435	434	433	422	420	blanc	DMC
¼X			◻	◺			·	◺	·	¼X
½X				⊙	·	✦	◖	◼	◼	½X
B'ST			◩						◪	B'ST

X	⬗	✳	◻	★	◁	X	I	▦	·	◯	X
DMC											DMC
801	783	782	780	762	760	758	754	746	727	DMC
¼X			◺	◺	◺			◺	▨	·	¼X
½X	◯					✦	▨	◖	◼	½X
B'ST								◩	◪	B'ST

X	▦	◪	◧	◑	◇	X	▦	·	◼	X
DMC										DMC
3064	3047	3046	3045	948	928	927	926	924	898	DMC
¼X	◺	◺	◺	◺	◺	◺	◺	◺	◺	¼X
½X		*	◼	◼		X	◻	◼	◇	◯	½X
B'ST								◪	◩	B'ST

X	◼	☆	I	◻	◉	✦	◻	X
DMC								DMC
3811	3810	3809	3808	3768	3328	3078	DMC
¼X			◺	◺			◺	¼X
½X						◻		½X
B'ST	◩			◪		◪		B'ST

Kreinik Fine Braid - 002
Pink area indicates last row of
top section of design.

Mary and Christ Child in Frame (shown on page 44): The design was stitched over 2 fabric threads on a 14" x 17" piece of Bone Lugana (25 ct). Three strands of floss or 1 strand of braid were used for Cross Stitch and 1 strand of floss or braid for Half Cross Stitch and Backstitch. It was custom framed.

Needlework adaptation by Donna Vermillion Giampa.

88

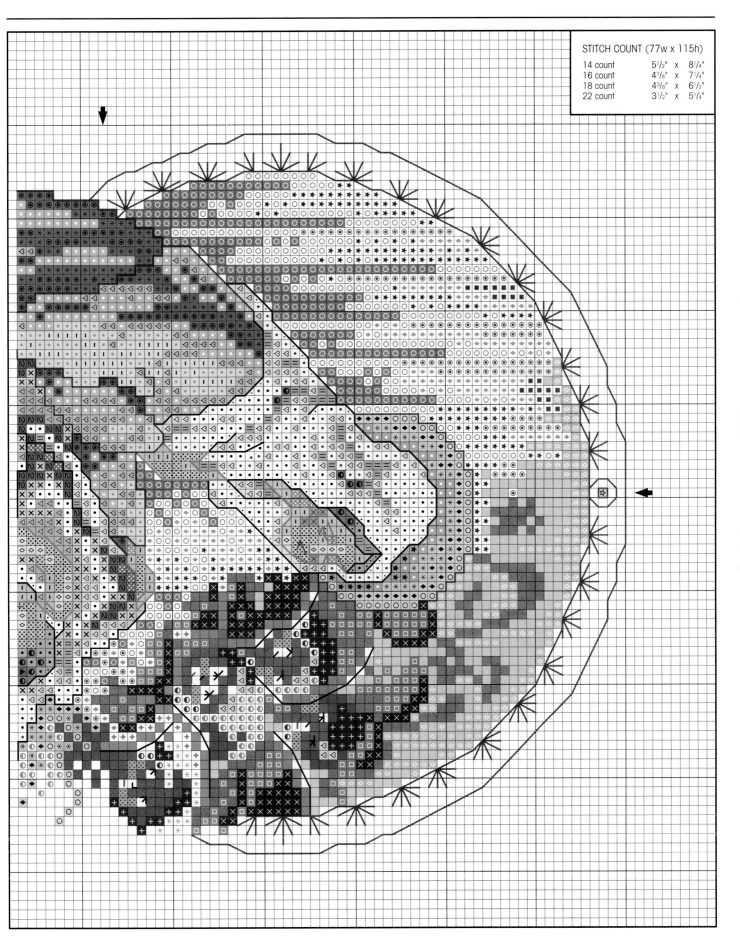

STITCH COUNT (77w x 115h)

14 count	5½"	x 8¼"
16 count	4⅞"	x 7¼"
18 count	4⅜"	x 6½"
22 count	3½"	x 5¼"

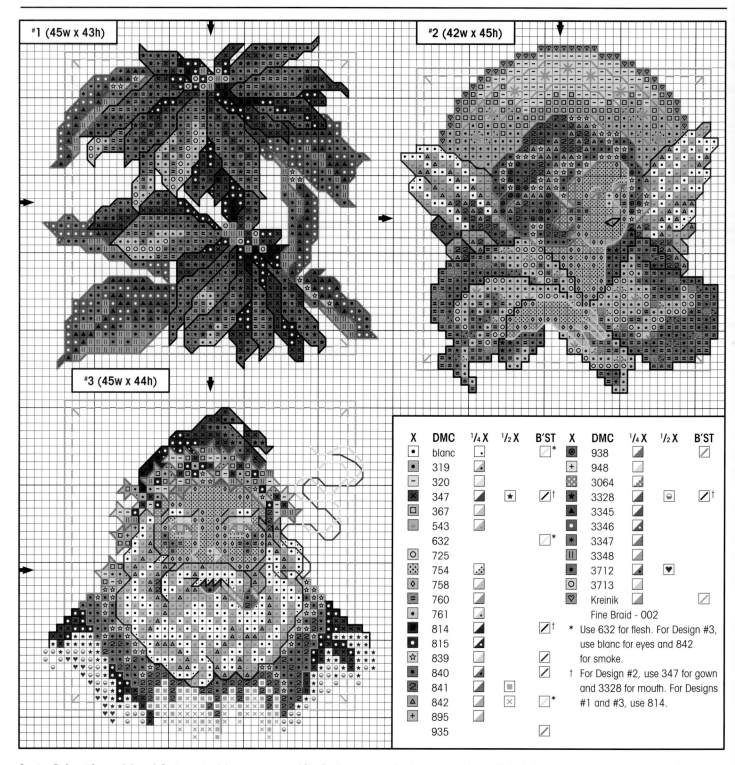

#1 (45w x 43h) **#2 (42w x 45h)** **#3 (45w x 44h)**

X	DMC	1/4 X	1/2 X	B'ST	X	DMC	1/4 X	1/2 X	B'ST
•	blanc	•		✓ *	◉	938	◤		✓
•	319	◤			+	948	◤		
–	320	◤				3064	◤		
✕	347	◤	★	✓ †	★	3328	◤	⊖	✓ †
▢	367	◤			▲	3345	◤		
	543	◤			●	3346	◤		
	632			✓ *	✳	3347	◤		
○	725				‖	3348	◤		
⠢	754	⠢			●	3712	◤	♥	
◇	758	◤			○	3713	◤		
≡	760	◤			♡	Kreinik	◤		✓
•	761	◤				Fine Braid - 002			
■	814	◤		✓ †					
◑	815	◤							
☆	839	◤		✓					
▪	840	◤		✓					
2	841	◤	▢	✓					
▲	842	◤	✕	✓ *					
+	895	◤							
	935			✓					

* Use 632 for flesh. For Design #3, use blanc for eyes and 842 for smoke.

† For Design #2, use 347 for gown and 3328 for mouth. For Designs #1 and #3, use 814.

Santa, Poinsettia, and Angel Ornaments (shown on page 42): Designs #1, #2, and #3 were each stitched over 2 fabric threads on an 8" square of Light Sand Cashel Linen® (28 ct). Three strands of floss were used for Cross Stitch and 1 strand of floss or braid for Half Cross Stitch and Backstitch.

For each ornament, you will need a 5" square of Light Sand Cashel Linen® for backing, two 3¹/₂" square pieces of adhesive mounting board, two 3¹/₂" square pieces of batting, 17" length of ¹/₄" dia. purchased cording with attached seam allowance, and clear-drying craft glue.

Centering design, trim stitched piece to measure 5" square.

Remove paper from one mounting board piece and press one batting piece onto mounting board. Repeat with remaining mounting board and batting.

Center wrong side of stitched piece over batting on one mounting board piece; fold edges of stitched piece to back of mounting board and glue in place. For ornament back, repeat with backing fabric and remaining mounting board.

Beginning and ending at bottom center of stitched piece, glue cording seam allowance to wrong side of ornament front, overlapping ends of cording. Matching wrong sides, glue ornament front and back together.

Needlework adaptations by Donna Vermillion Giampa.

STITCH COUNT (87w x 70h)			
14 count	6¼"	x	5"
16 count	5½"	x	4⅜"
18 count	4⅞"	x	4"
22 count	4"	x	3¼"

X	DMC	B'ST
♥ *	225 &	
	761	
▢	347	
▪	725	
•	760	
▫ *	760 &	
	761	
2	761	
■	814	╱
▥	815	
✕	3328	╱
	3345	╱
▽	3347	
+	3348	

* Use 2 strands of first floss color listed and 1 strand of second floss color listed.

Poinsettia Pillow (shown on page 43): The design was stitched over 2 fabric threads on a 15" x 14" piece of Cream Lugana (25 ct). Three strands of floss were used for Cross Stitch and 1 strand for Backstitch.

For pillow, you will need a 10½" x 9¼" piece of fabric for backing, 7" x 72" fabric strip for ruffle (pieced as necessary), 40" length of ⅜" dia. purchased cording with attached seam allowance, and polyester fiberfill.

Centering design, trim stitched piece to measure 10½" x 9¼".

If needed, trim seam allowance of cording to ½"; pin cording to right side of stitched piece, making a ⅜" clip in seam allowance of cording at corners. Ends of cording should overlap approximately 4". Turn overlapped ends of cording toward outside edge of stitched piece; baste cording to stitched piece.

For ruffle, press short edges of fabric strip ½" to wrong side. Matching wrong sides and long edges, fold strip in half; press. Machine baste ½" from raw edges; gather

fabric strip to fit stitched piece. Matching raw edges, pin ruffle to right side of stitched piece overlapping short ends ¼". Use a ½" seam allowance to sew ruffle to stitched piece.

Matching right sides and leaving an opening for turning, use a ½" seam allowance to sew stitched piece and backing fabric together. Trim seam allowances diagonally at corners; turn pillow right side out, carefully pushing corners outward. Stuff pillow with polyester fiberfill and blind stitch opening closed.

Poinsettia Sweater (shown on page 47): The design was stitched over an 11" x 10" piece of 12 mesh waste canvas on a purchased sweater with top of design 1" below bottom of neckband. Three strands of floss were used for Cross Stitch and 1 strand for Backstitch. See Working on Waste Canvas, page 95.

Needlework adaptation by Linda Culp Calhoun.

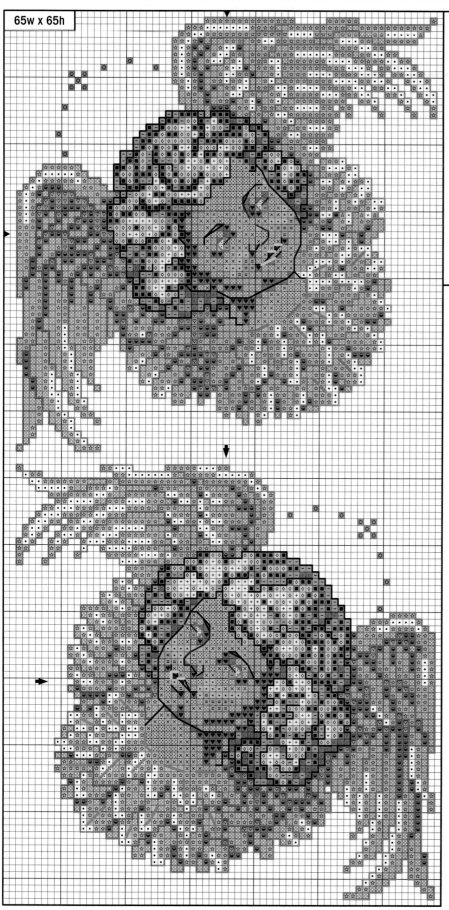

65w x 65h

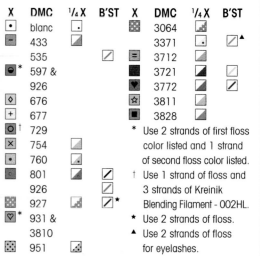

X	DMC	¼ X	B'ST	X	DMC	¼ X	B'ST
•	blanc	•		▦	3064	◩	
▬	433	◩			3371	•	◩ ▲
	535		◺	═	3712	◩	
◉ *	597 &			■	3721	◨	◺
	926			♥	3772	◨	◺
◇	676			☆	3811	◩	
+	677			■	3828	◩	
◎ †	729						
✕	754	◺		* Use 2 strands of first floss			
•	760	◿		color listed and 1 strand			
◪	801	◩	◺	of second floss color listed.			
	926		◺	† Use 1 strand of floss and			
▦	927	◿	◺ ★	3 strands of Kreinik			
♥ *	931 &			Blending Filament - 002HL.			
	3810			★ Use 2 strands of floss.			
▦	951	◿		▲ Use 2 strands of floss			
				for eyelashes.			

Angel Wreath (shown on page 40): The designs were each stitched over 2 fabric threads on a 9" square of Light Sand Cashel Linen® (28 ct). Three strands of floss were used for Cross Stitch and 1 strand for Backstitch, unless otherwise noted in the color key.

For each ornament, you will need a 9" square piece of felt for backing, tracing paper, pencil, 7½" square piece of adhesive mounting board, 7½" square piece of batting, 4" length of ½" dia. cord, 56" length of 2½"w wire-edge ribbon, decorated 20" dia. wreath, and clear-drying craft glue.

For pattern, fold tracing paper in half and place fold on dashed line of Ornament Pattern, page 96; trace pattern onto tracing paper. Cut out pattern; unfold and press flat. Draw around pattern once on mounting board, once on batting, and once on felt; cut out. Remove paper from mounting board and press batting piece onto mounting board.

Referring to photo, position pattern on wrong side of stitched piece; pin pattern in place. Cut stitched piece **1" larger** than pattern on all sides. Clip ½" into edge of stitched piece at ½" intervals. Center wrong side of stitched piece over batting on mounting board piece; fold edges of stitched piece to back of mounting board and glue in place. Glue felt backing to wrong side of ornament. Referring to photo, glue one end of cord to wrong side of ornament. Tie ribbon in a bow and glue to top of cord. Referring to photo, glue ornaments and bows to wreath.

Needlework adaptation by Sandy Orton.

X	DMC	¼X	½X	B'ST
•	blanc	•		
※*	blanc		■†	
◼	315	◢		╱★
◉	316	◢		╱★
◼	347	◢		╱▲
⊞	420	◢		
□	422	◢		
+	433	◢		
2	520	◢		
•	522	◢		
=	523	◢		
○	524	◢		
▽	597	◢		
●	598	◢		
	632			╱
★	640	◢	★	
◼	642	◢	2	
▲	644	◢	◆	
△	725	□		
•	727	•		
‖	747	□		
▧	754	▨		
−	758	◢		
◼	761	◢		
✕	778	◢		
✕	782	◢		
◼	783	▨		
▽	801	◢		╱°
○	819	◢		
●	822	◢	H	
	869			╱▲
✳	898		◉	╱▲
	924		=	
	926		▲	
	927		8	
	928		○	
◆	935	◢		
◇	948	□		
◼	3045	◢		
◉	3046	◢		
☆	3047	◢		
▨	3064	◢		
○	3078	◢		
◼	3328	◢		
★	3363			
□	3712	◢		
	3721			╱★
▽	3726	◢		
‖	3727	◢		
	3768		☆	
	3790		✳	╱°
8	3808			╱
☆	3809	◢		
•	3810	◢		
✳	3811	◢		
2	Kreinik Very Fine Braid - 002			╱

* Use 3 strands of floss and 1 strand of Kreinik Blending Filament - 032 for tree.

† Use 1 strand of floss and 1 strand of Kreinik Blending Filament - 032.
★ Use 347 for apples. Use 3721 for mouths.

Use 315 for all other.
▲ Use 420 for eyebrows.
Use 869 for hair. Use 898 for all other.

Project Information on page 94.
° Use 3790 for wings.
Use 801 for all other.

93

CHRISTMAS

Christmas Angels Album (shown on page 45, chart on page 93). The design was stitched over 2 fabric threads on a 14" x 17" piece of Cream Cashel Linen® (28 ct). Three strands of floss were used for Cross Stitch and 1 strand for Half Cross Stitch and Backstitch, unless otherwise noted in the color key.

For album, you will need a 9¹/₂" x 11¹/₂" photo album with a 2¹/₂" spine, 1 yard of 44"w fabric, 22" x 11¹/₂" piece of batting for album, 6¹/₂" x 9¹/₂" piece of batting for stitched piece, two 9" x 11" pieces of poster board, 6¹/₂" x 9¹/₂" piece of mounting board, 34" length of ¹/₂"w gold trim, and clear-drying craft glue.

Centering design, trim stitched piece to measure 8¹/₂" x 11¹/₂".

Cut two 3" x 11" strips of fabric. Glue one long edge of one strip ¹/₄" under one long side of metal spine inside album; glue remaining edges of strip to album. Repeat with remaining strip and long side of metal spine; allow to dry.

Glue batting to outside of album. Cut a 24" x 13¹/₂" piece of fabric for outside of album.

Center album, batting side down, on wrong side of fabric; fold fabric at corners to inside of album and glue in place. At center bottom of album, turn a 4" section of fabric ¹/₄" to wrong side (**Fig. 1**); glue folded edge under spine of album. Repeat at center top of album. Fold remaining edges of fabric to inside of album and glue in place; allow to dry.

Fig. 1

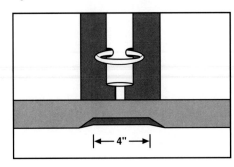

Cut two 11" x 13" pieces of fabric for inside covers. Center one piece of poster board on wrong side of one piece of fabric; fold edges of fabric to back of poster board and glue in place. Glue wrong side of covered poster board to inside of front cover of album approximately ¹/₄" from top, bottom, and outside edges of album. Repeat with remaining piece of fabric and poster board for inside back cover.

To mount stitched piece, glue batting to mounting board. Center stitched piece on batting and fold edges of stitched piece to back of mounting board; glue in place. Center and glue wrong side of mounted stitched piece to front cover.

Beginning at lower right corner of stitched piece, glue gold trim around outside edge of stitched piece; trim ends.

*Needlework adaptation by
Donna Vermillion Giampa.*

94

GENERAL INSTRUCTIONS

WORKING WITH CHARTS

How to Read Charts: Each of the designs is shown in chart form. Each colored square on the chart represents one Cross Stitch or one Half Cross Stitch. Each colored triangle on the chart represents one One-Quarter Stitch or one Three-Quarter Stitch. In some charts, reduced symbols are used to indicate One-Quarter Stitches (**Fig. 1**). **Fig. 2** and **Fig. 3** indicate Cross Stitch under Backstitch.

Fig. 1	**Fig. 2**	**Fig. 3**

Black or colored dots on the chart represent Cross Stitch, French Knots, or bead placement. The black or colored straight lines on the chart indicate Backstitch. The symbol is omitted or reduced when a French Knot or Backstitch covers a square.

Each chart is accompanied by a color key. This key indicates the color of floss to use for each stitch on the chart. The headings on the color key are for Cross Stitch (**X**), DMC color number (**DMC**), One-Quarter Stitch (**¼X**), Three-Quarter Stitch (**¾X**), Half Cross Stitch (**½X**), and Backstitch (**B'ST**). Color key columns should be read vertically and horizontally to determine type of stitch and floss color. Some designs may include stitches worked with metallic thread, such as blending filament or braid. The metallic thread may be blended with floss or used alone. If any metallic thread is used in a design, the color key will contain the necessary information.

STITCHING TIPS

Working over Two Fabric Threads: Use the sewing method instead of the stab method when working over two fabric threads. To use the sewing method, keep your stitching hand on the right side of the fabric (instead of stabbing the fabric with the needle and taking your stitching hand to the back of the fabric to pick up the needle). With the sewing method, you take the needle down and up with one stroke instead of two. To add support to stitches, it is important that the first Cross Stitch be placed on the fabric with stitch 1-2 beginning and ending where a vertical fabric thread crosses over a horizontal fabric thread (**Fig. 4**). When the first stitch is in the correct position, the entire design will be placed properly, with vertical fabric threads supporting each stitch.

Fig. 4

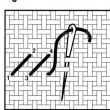

Attaching Beads: Refer to chart for bead placement and sew bead in place using a fine needle that will pass through bead. Bring needle up at 1, run needle through bead and then down at 2. Secure floss on back or move to next bead as shown in **Fig. 5**.

Fig. 5

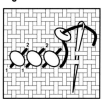

Working on Waste Canvas: Waste canvas is a special canvas that provides an evenweave grid for placing stitches on fabric. After the design is worked over the canvas, the canvas threads are removed, leaving the design on the fabric. The canvas is available in several mesh sizes.

Cover edges of canvas with masking tape. Cut a piece of lightweight non-fusible interfacing the same size as canvas to provide a firm stitching base.

Find desired stitching area and mark center of area with a pin. Match center of canvas to pin. Use the blue threads in canvas to place canvas straight on garment; pin canvas to garment. Pin interfacing to wrong side of garment. Baste all layers together as shown in **Fig. 6**.

Using a sharp needle, work design, stitching from large holes to large holes. Trim canvas to within ¾" of design. Dampen canvas until it becomes limp. Pull out canvas threads one at a time using tweezers (**Fig. 7**). Trim interfacing close to design.

Fig. 6 **Fig. 7**

STITCH DIAGRAMS

Note: Bring threaded needle up at 1 and all odd numbers and down at 2 and all even numbers.

Counted Cross Stitch (X): Work one Cross Stitch to correspond to each colored square on the chart. For horizontal rows, work stitches in two journeys (**Fig. 8**). For vertical rows, complete each stitch as shown (**Fig. 9**). When working over two fabric threads, work Cross Stitch as shown in **Fig. 10**. When the chart shows a Backstitch crossing a colored square (**Fig. 11**), a Cross Stitch should be worked first; then the Backstitch (**Fig. 16** or **17**) should be worked on top of the Cross Stitch.

Fig. 8 **Fig. 9**

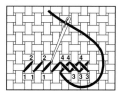 

Fig. 10 **Fig. 11**

Quarter Stitch (¼X and ¾X): Quarter Stitches are denoted by triangular shapes of color on the chart and on the color key. For a One-Quarter Stitch, come up at 1 (**Fig. 12**), then split fabric thread to go down at 2. When stitches 1-4 are worked in the same color, the resulting stitch is called a Three-Quarter Stitch (**¾X**). **Fig. 13** shows the technique for Quarter Stitches when working over two fabric threads.

Fig. 12 **Fig. 13**

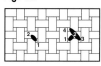

Half Cross Stitch (½X): This stitch is one journey of the Cross Stitch and is worked from lower left to upper right as shown in **Fig. 14**. When working over two fabric threads, work Half Cross Stitch as shown in **Fig. 15**.

Fig. 14 **Fig. 15**

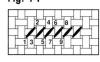

Backstitch (B'ST): For outline detail, Backstitch (shown on chart and on color key by black or colored straight lines) should be worked after the design has been completed (**Fig. 16**). When working over two fabric threads, work Backstitch as shown in **Fig. 17**.

Fig. 16 **Fig. 17**

 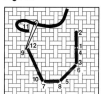

Continued on page 96.

French Knot: Bring needle up at 1. Wrap floss once around needle and insert needle at 2, holding end of floss with non-stitching fingers (**Fig. 18**). Tighten knot, then pull needle through fabric, holding floss until it must be released. For larger knot, use more strands of floss; wrap only once.

Fig. 18

Lazy Daisy Stitch: Bring needle up at 1 and make a loop. Go down at 1 and come up at 2, keeping floss below point of needle (**Fig. 19**). Pull needle through and go down at 2 to anchor loop, completing stitch. (**Note:** To support stitches, it may be helpful to go down in edge of next fabric thread when anchoring loop.)

Fig. 19

Blanket Stitch: Knot one end of floss. Bri needle up from wrong side at 1, even w edge of fabric. Go down at 2 and co up at 3, keeping floss below point needle (**Fig. 20**). Continue to stitch in t manner, keeping tension even and stitch evenly spaced (**Fig. 21**).

Fig. 20

Fig. 21

Top

**Ornament Pattern
(instructions on page 92)**

**Scissors Case Pattern
(instructions on page 67)**

Instructions tested and photo items made by L
Allen, Debbie Anderson, Lisa Arey, Kandi Ashf
Muriel Hicks, Pat Johnson, Wanda J. Linsley, Ph
Lundy, Susan McDonald, Pamela Nash, Tam
Necessary, Linda L. Nelson, Patricia O'Neil, Rebe
K. Parsons, Laura Rowan, Cynthia Sanders, Steph
Gail Sharp, Lavonne Sims, Lorissa Smith, He
Stanton, Amy Taylor, Trish Vines,
Andrea Westbrook.

96